To Brigux

Roseanne
4/24/19

New Home Sales
& Marketing
Best Practices

Kerry Mulcrone

For general information on our other products and services,
please call 612-817-4089.

Kerry@kerryandco.com

www.kerryandco.com

ISBN-13: 978-1727238921
ISBN-10: 1727238923

DEDICATION

This book was thoughtfully designed with all my Builders, VP's of Sales and Marketing, Marketing Directors, Sales Managers and of course my Sales Friends in mind. Without all of you there would be no KerryandCo, and I do not take that lightly. Enjoy and stay perpetual learners!

ACKNOWLEDGEMENTS

Thank you to Janelle Dachtera and Debra Kastner for their efforts to edit and put this book together, and to my friends in the New Home Sales industry for their unique chapter contributions.

CONTENTS

Introduction

I will start at the very beginning. I don't want you to have to wonder or guess what this book is all about.

A memory came to me in the middle of the night, which is a fairly regular occurrence for me. Some of my best ideas and work is a result of these moments.

Let me take you back to an International Builders Show a few years ago. While perusing Builder Books, admittedly to spy on how many copies of my book were still on the shelf, I overheard a conversation. "There are so many good books, I wish they were all in one so I didn't have to pick and choose."

Welcome to my dream! I will gather some of my industry friends and together we will put that book in writing.

I give you New Home Sales & Marketing Best Practices. This book is about both principles and nuances that matter so much in the New Home Industry. Each chapter is different and unique to its author.

Enjoy and get your pens ready, this is a "noteworthy" book to catapult you and your business to a new level!

Kerry Mulcrone is a National Builder Consultant, Sales Trainer and Speaker. She has over 30 years of proven sales success, both onsite and in new home sales management. She has a knowledge of how profitable organizations operate, "from the inside out", and combined with this knowledge and her strengths as an educator, she works with companies beginning with company leadership to customer-focused sales training. Her energetic and positive approach provides a powerful catalyst for developing company synergy and sales systems that create a "we love to work here" environment. Her fresh and unique "hands on" approach has gained her recognition from well-known companies and successful building organizations from coast to coast!

In addition to her onsite work, she is an accomplished motivational speaker/trainer, with appearances at International Builder's Shows, Local Home Builder Associations, and numerous industry conferences and workshops. Kerry has attained several prestigious designations including the NAHB Member of the Institute of Residential Marketing (MIRM), Certified New Home Sales Professional (CSP), and the Certified Marketing Professional (CMP). She is a regular contributor to local and national industry publications, and she is a published author including *Model Home Model Store, Think Retail*, and *Think Retail 2.0, Closing the Sale*.

When Kerry is not pouring her heart and soul into her work, she is sharing them with her family and her 2 grandchildren, ages 12 and 5. You can contact Kerry by email at Kerry@KerryandCo.com, or check out her website at www.KerryandCo.com.

Positioning for Success

Have you ever felt as if you were presenting your model home in a way you thought was valuable and helpful to the prospective buyer, and yet the level of engagement and response you received from them was just so-so?

Consider this. Maybe it wasn't the information causing that ho-hum reaction and response, but rather how you were presenting it--and even more importantly, where and when you were presenting it! It's all about the emotional connection created between you and the customer at every juncture which creates their response. This emotional connection is a combination of many factors, both intrinsic and extrinsic. How someone feels inside creates a spark which promotes an outward engagement to a level where they hear and respond positively. I am talking about perfected and positioned model presentations which bring out the best in customers.

To better understand exactly where I am going with this, let's define *Personal Positioning*. It is the art of presenting your best self and the best features of the model home, all at the right time and place, in the right way, with the right message.

Whew, that is a mouthful. However, those very words will take you to the next level in new home sales. *Personal Positioning* separates the *salesperson* from the *sales specialist*, as I like to refer to them. Positioning doesn't come as easy as you may think. It's a conscious decision on your part. However, when accomplished, it creates, as Disney would say, *A Magical Experience*.

Yes, who you are, where you stand and where your customer stands makes a huge difference in what they see and connect to what you are saying. Let's start at the very beginning with this *Personal Positioning Strategy* and begin with YOU!

Step #1

Before you ever leave home, position yourself each day with the right attitude and your best professional appearance. First impressions happen in just a matter of seconds and you only get one chance to make a good first impression. Your appearance, along with your welcoming smile and knowledge as a sales specialist, make all the difference between a positive, a negative or no connection with the customer. It sounds crazy that I even have to mention that but believe me, it is a conscious decision when you begin your day and it is sometimes overlooked. The way you positively promote yourself, your company, your homes and your community determines the potential of a *magic experience* happening. So you see, you are placing yourself in the position of having the most potential by starting the sales process before you ever leave your own door to open your model door or office door. Check and double check...are you ready to help a customer purchase a home today?

Step #2

Did you do your homework? Is someone coming to visit you today? What have you done in terms of calling, emailing, following up with your pipeline and physically visiting realtors to ensure they all know how to find you, when to find you, where to find you and most importantly why they should find you? Is your model neat, orderly and appealing from the curb, through the front door and beyond? It's all about pre-model preparation that makes for successful, fun days.

Step #3

Your doors are open to your model home and a visitor walks in. How do you greet them, and what do they see based on where you are standing? Your placement is critical to beginning your time together--it is the first chance for you to make a positive emotional connection. Where you stand is crucial because it places your visitor where they have an amazing vantage point of what your model offers and from which they may become intrigued. Don't let them look at blank walls, untidy or copious paperwork or tight foyers. Direct their eye at interesting displays if you are in a Sales Center or eye-capturing interior views if walking directly into the home. Make sure your opening position is not random and is choreographed by you so each and every time a valuable new customer comes in, they feel the sense that they belong there and with you. Is your opening position when a customer enters your model currently the very best place for them to have the fabulous vantage point of seeing things which excite them?

Step #4

Once you have greeted your visitor, welcomed them to your model and you move through your tour, position your customer to see all the places and spaces in a home in the very best light. Your planned presentation and demonstration, coupled with your needs analysis and discovery questions, will promote emotional connections to both words and design! Remember, they will follow where you lead or guide them. A few hints:

- If the space is rather tight, the customer belongs in the space--you don't. Guide them with your words, sending them in to experience things from your direction and not your physical presence. Make sure your visitors are seeing the best view of the model, both inside and out. Make sure they stand and face a window which has a magnificent view.

- Always have what I call *homework assignments*, which have them looking for special features and benefits the builder has thoughtfully designed into the home. Guide them to see these features and benefits most important to them. This helps people experience everything there is to see, rather than just a glance and out the front door.

- Demonstrate and position the customer both forwards and backwards in their tour. By this, I mean there are things to be viewed as you move forward through the model, but there are also great vantage points to see as they walk away into other spaces and places. Where you go they will follow. Where you lead and guide will help them take in the home in its best light. It is a little bit of a show. You are the actors and actresses, the customers are the audience and your home is the stage.

- Positioning is matching powerful statements in powerful places! So, I ask you, where along the way do you add your builder integrity statements? Where do you show energy features? Where do you use homeowner's testimonial statements? Where do you use the power of the pause and just settle in and chat? Where do you go from interior to exterior features? Remember, if it has a $ *Dollar Value* in the price of the home it has a $ *Presentation Value* in the placement of the customer.

Creating your Value Wedge

When I teach positioning, I also include *Positioning Statements*. We all know there is a lot of overlap in what we do in the home-building industry. However, there are very distinctive differences amongst individual companies, which are their personal differentiators. You should focus on what you can do for the customer that is different from what your competition does. That is your *Value Wedge*. Your *Value Wedge* must be unique to you and defensible. It also should be presented in a timely and meaningful way throughout your presentation. It is not a piece of marketing collateral handed out in a packet at the end of a visit. Your *Value Wedge* is what you say best in the places you know best which deliver impact and involvement.

The Sale is in the Story

Story Positioning is about telling your company's story in a way that encourages emotional involvement with customers so they want to learn more and ask questions. The challenge is, many New Home Sales Specialists tell the story in a way that doesn't differentiate their company enough. To create a powerful perception of value in your stories, you need to tell the *before* and the *after*. You need to show contrast! When you tell builder and customer testimonial stories, don't be afraid to link data with emotion. Sometimes the best way to talk about the story is to talk about the company, the people who were affected in various ways and how it became a great thing in the end, how the company and the lives of other customers became better, stronger, more fun after overcoming adversity. Where did the company start? What were its humble beginnings? What did the customer object to and then felt differently? Always remember *Once Upon a Time...and They All Lived Happily Ever After* resonates with all of us!

Make your Customer the Hero

Positioning someone to be the hero or heroine is a talent. You do not need to win--they do. The customer needs to save their day, not always you! Your role as the presenter is that of a mentor. You are there to help your customer see what can change in their world. Realize you are part of how that can happen. I train salespeople to be the solution to the discontent someone is currently feeling. But let me be clear, the magic is when they become their own hero in realizing what that solution is, and you were a key player in establishing that solution.

Competing in the Cook- off Challenge

When you position yourself against your competitors in the end you are competing in a *Competition Cook-off*. It's a specification war! You might win on one included feature, but then the competition meets that feature and raises you one. In that process, you are positioning your competition, not yourself. You are both having a similar dialogue with the customer which can lead to the fatal *no decision at all*. Instead, position your conversations to talk about "Why us?" and "Why now?" and "Why here?" Challenge the customer status quo of feature shopping and instead consider your truly unique value and differentiators. Don't get me wrong...know your competition as well as you know your company, but shed it in a light that causes movement to action not movement to confusion and concession.

Service Positioning

You are positioned with service in the mind of the customer when you create value to them in their mind which makes you stand out amongst their other choices. Service is wide in description but paramount in a customer's eyes.

Service is not a department...it is not warranty...it is a way of thinking from top down.

1) Convenience--Making things easy for them.
2) Care--Providing friendly and diligent service that is pleasing and prompt.
3) Reliability--Being there on time when they need you.
4) Performance--Doing what you do in the best way you can do it.
5) Tailoring--Meeting the different needs in different circumstances.
6) Authenticity--Being the Real Deal.
7) Reputation--Having a track record that speaks for itself.
8) Legacy--Positioning yourself for creating a history in your company.
9) Knowledge--Knowing what you are doing and instilling confidence.
10) Gratitude--Being a company that appreciates your customer's business.

Strengthen your Position by Practicing Attraction and Action Strategies

At the very core of attraction and connecting is this--where you place your thoughts, energy, intention and knowledge defines what you create in any given moment. This is not some magical or crazy power. In fact, the guiding principle of attracting what you want is simple. Combine mental, emotional and positive energy with physical action and you can make amazing things happen, like helping people to see things in the best light for both considering working with you and ultimately purchasing from you! It is the physical action of moving your customers into the place of most potential where they can see, hear and feel the strongest messages. I call this *Positioning for Success.*

Take a moment ...

Do you refresh and rehearse your model presentation?

Are you planning and preparing to tell your company's story?

Are you personally positioned for success?

Meredith Oliver, CSP, MIRM, is the founder and creative director of Meredith Communications, a digital marketing agency in Raleigh, NC specializing in home builder marketing. Meredith Communications is in its sixteenth year delivering digital marketing solutions such as website design, search engine optimization, and social media marketing. Meredith holds a Masters Degree in Communication Technology from Rollins College and is the author of three books, 1) Click Power: The Proven System Home Builders Use to Drive More Traffic, Leads and Sales and 2) FANtastic Marketing: Leverage Your Fan Factor, Build a Blockbuster Brand, Score New Customers, and Knock Out the Competition and 3) FANtastic Selling: The 10 Undeniable Traits of Rock-Star, Top-Producing, Quota-Busting Salespeople.

She has been speaking professionally for 15 years and holds the prestigious CSP designation, the highest designation conferred by the National Speakers Association. She is a seventeen-time presenter at the National Association of Home Builders' (NAHB) International Builders Show including multiple appearances in the Super Sales Rally.

Meredith holds the MIRM and the MCSP designations. She is an approved instructor for both designations.

Meredith lives in Raleigh, NC with her husband, son, and three Shih Tzus. She loves what she does and can't imagine doing anything else. You can follow her on Twitter @MeredithCSP and on Instagram @MeredithsShoes22.

Is Your Website FANtastic?
Six Slam Dunk Tips to Drive More Sales with Your Online Presence

Your website is the foundation of your sales and marketing strategy. According to a 2016 Bokka Group Buyer Conversion Study, 90 percent of home shoppers use the Internet during their home search, and 81 percent want to see interactive floor plans and virtual tours on builder websites. A 2017 Redfin survey found that 35 percent of homebuyers bid on a home sight-unseen, up from 19 percent in June 2016.

On a scale of one to ten, how well are you meeting the needs of your home shoppers as they peruse your online presence? After browsing your website, do home buyers feel compelled to buy one of your homes sight-unseen?

Your website is the most essential tool in your sales and marketing toolbox. Knowing this fact, it is imperative that you go from a good website to a great website. The true mark of an outstanding website isn't the graphics or the copy, it is the percentage of leads the site converts.

Ultimately, you want to make sales, correct? Then the accurate measure of an effective site must be lead conversion. An outstanding home builder website converts 1 – 2 percent of unique visitors into a lead. Leads can take several forms - including an email request for information, a live chat, a phone call, a social media inquiry or a text request for more information.

In this chapter, I am going to give you six FANtastic tips to make your website a lead-converting machine. Your website doesn't have to be a passive, static, online brochure which is a hassle to update and doesn't generate leads. Your website can be a very active sales vehicle which drives as much as 40 percent of your total sales each year.

Tip #1 – Commit to a FAN Centric Website

A FANtastic website is a website that is *about* the fans and *for* the fans.

It's not about you. What?! It's my website. How is it not about me? (I can hear you thinking it!)

In today's digital world, we are more connected than ever and we are more distracted than ever. We selectively pay attention to marketing messages because of the vast amount of information coming into our brains on a daily basis. Billboards, bumper stickers, direct mail, radio, television, email and social media are all blasting on high every single day. We are deluged with information.

With all the beeping and buzzing it's a wonder we pay attention to anything. However, we do - out of hardwired desire to connect and belong, we choose to pay attention to the messages and brands that connect with us. We choose to tune into the people, companies and products that speak to us on an emotional level.

So your builder website needs to be FANtastic. I have capitalized the letters FAN in the word to symbolize that the FANS must come first in your marketing and on your website.

Think about your favorite websites. What do you love about them? Why do you visit them frequently and cyber-stalk them, reading all of the content and downloading free offerings? Because they resonate with you. You feel a connection and you feel like that brand gets you.

Does your builder website demonstrate through the copy, graphics, interactive tools and navigation structure that you understand your FANS?

Why am I using the term FANS to describe your potential home buyers when they haven't purchased a home from you yet? Simple. As a home buyer researches possible new homes, they become invested during the process. Whether the moving time frame is immediate and they need a quick move-in or they start researching a year in advance, as they browse, view virtual tours, scroll through photo galleries and read FAQ blog posts, they became excited and empowered to buy. As discussed in my book *FANtastic Marketing: Leverage Your Fan Factor, Build a Blockbuster Brand, Score New Customers, and Wipe Out the Competition*, on average, a person will visit a site a minimum of eleven times before they will commit to seeking more information from a home builder. It is easy to conclude that after eleven visits to your website--and especially if they have reached out via live chat, email, phone, or walk-in--they are a FAN of your homes!

Are you committed to a FANtastic website? Are you willing to do what it takes to make the site useful to your FANS so you can sell more homes? Great! Move on to tip #2.

Tip #2 – Deliver FANtastic Visual Content

Your website visitors are looking for FANtastic visual content. They want to be informed, educated and inspired – visually. Think about it.

As a society we have entered into what many may believe is the age of text overload. We have text messages, site updates, social media postings and email that are continually blasted at us throughout the day. Text overload has caused people to stop reading long blocks of text and to start scanning for sound bites and bullet points. Copy or blocks of text don't capture our interest. We only stop to pay attention if something has visual appeal.

There's an old saying that is still just as true today...*pictures are worth a thousand words*. Visuals are a short-cut to help us comprehend complex information quickly and efficiently. Home buyers are looking for visual content that is easy to understand

and illustrates what is unique and special about your homes.

At Meredith Communications, we actively monitor the Google Analytics reports for approximately thirty-five home builder websites every month. If you aren't familiar with Google Analytics, it is a free Google product that provides real-time tracking of your website's performance. Think of it like an EKG for your website.

We see the same patterns every month with regards to what content receives the most clicks and generates the most leads. Without fail, it's the pages with the highest use of visual content-- typically the Our Communities Page, the Community Profile Pages, Model Home Detail Pages, Floor Plan Detail Pages and Available Home Detail Pages. To identify which pages on your website receive the most visits, review the Top Pages report in Google Analytics. Look not only for the pages that received the highest volume of visits, but also the pages that had the longest visit length, lowest bounce rate and highest lead conversion.

The builders who have invested in high-impact visuals, such as professional photography, 3D renderings, interactive floor plans, interactive sitemaps, video and virtual tours have the longest average site visits and lead conversion rates.

If you are already doing the basics with your digital marketing, consider spending more time and budget on creating top-flight online content. You can use it to make your website more effective and you can re-purpose it in your social media pages and email marketing efforts.

Tip #3 – Optimize Your Site for Google

Step three to creating a FANtastic website is to make sure that the number one potential traffic source on the web, Google, can find and index your site. Prospective home buyers are searching for new homes and home builders on Google, and you want to appear on page one or the top of page two for those searches.

The irony of optimizing your site for Google is that Google relies on written content to index your site. So, while you don't need paragraphs of text for your FANS because they prefer visuals, you do need strategically written and optimized text for the Google algorithm.

Your written content should contain relevant keyword phrases that home buyers use to search for homes on Google. We optimize thirty-to-forty home builder websites per month, and regardless of the market, the most commonly-searched relevant keyword phrases for home builders are variations of *new homes, home builders* and *homes for sale.*

On-site optimization usually takes expert help. Google changes their algorithms often which makes staying current on the latest requirements a full-time job.

You might be thinking that search engine optimization is counterintuitive to the FANtastic concept. It may sound like optimizing your site for Google is all about YOU and not the FANS. We believe that making your website easy for a home shopper to find you is making it about them. We know from Google's keyword tool that home shoppers are looking for *new homes* and *home builders* in your area. How easy are you to find?

Of course, you want to approach your on-site search engine optimization with moderation and always keep your FANS in mind. Don't overdo the keyword usage. Make sure your website is user-friendly with intuitive navigation and is mobile-friendly. Doing these things is called usability – making your website about the FANS. Usability is a major ranking factor in Google's algorithm.

Tip #4 – Manage Your Website with a FANtastic CMS

The next important step for a FANtastic website is to make sure that you have the right Content Management System (CMS) in place so you can easily make your site FANtastic. To harness the real power of your website to drive leads and sales, update and manage the site in-house on a daily basis. Asking your webmaster to make all of your website changes can be expensive and not as timely as doing them yourself. Unless you want to learn to code, the most efficient way to manage a site is with a user-friendly CMS. A CMS allows you to edit, add, and subtract content on your site from the convenience of your office without knowing HTML code. If you can book a hotel room online or send out an email in MailChimp, you can use a CMS.

There are many CMS options available, and they range from free, open-source to high-end proprietary custom platforms. At Meredith Communications, we developed a customized version of WordPress specifically for home builders. WordPress is a top-rated, prevalent, open source CMS platform which is easy to use. Of course, you can use any management system you want, but it is generally agreed on by most in the website management world that WordPress is the easiest to use and the most compatible with newly-designed sites. We have also found the Google search algorithm responds very well to WordPress sites.

In addition to being user-friendly, you want a CMS that allows you to access all of the content on your site. The more access you have to your site, the better, because it puts you in control of the site instead of being so reliant on your webmaster. You may never access certain more technical parts of the site, but it's crucial that you or whatever digital marketing company you hire can access it if needed. Next time you sign an agreement to build a website, make sure the agreement states you have the rights for the front-end design AND the back-end CMS files. Most website development contracts give you the rights to the graphic design files on the front-end of your website, the part of the site which is seen by the public. The designer often retains the rights to the backend because they want to charge you a monthly management fee after the site launches.

Owning both your front and back-end of your site allows you to move your site to another hosting or management company if you desire. Web management companies go out of business, needs for the site expand and may no longer be met by the current provider or you may find a better deal. Whatever the reason you have to move your site at a later date, you want to make sure that you own everything on that site so you are not forced to start over once your site is established.

Tip #5 – Blog Your Way to More Traffic & Leads

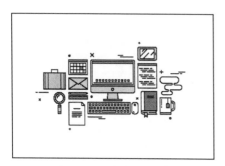

The next thing necessary for a FANtastic website is a blog. Your blog can be used to generate interest in your company in a very non-salesy way. Google also really loves blog content, especially if it is done correctly, because it adds valuable information to your website. Additionally, Google will rank your site higher if you regularly contribute to the blog so the information stays fresh.

So the next question is, what makes a good blog? Well, there are several things you can do that will draw attention to your blog and your main site, as well. The first thing you want to do with your blog is create a list of interesting subjects you feel are beneficial to your home buyers but are not solely promoting buying one of your homes.

For example, you may want to write a post about the five things that make moving to a new home easier. Pick subjects about the local area surrounding your communities. You may want to write about the five best places to take your family for a picnic or the top three seafood restaurants in your area. Write a post about unique entertainment venues, new dining experiences and local recreation areas. Write posts about what you need to register for school in your area, how to change your address online, or even when the local grocery stores run their sales. All of these topics contain essential information about a community that will draw people to the blog and once on the blog, to your community, floor plan and available homes pages.

A blog post should be between 300 and 500 words long. Break up the text to make it easy to read, and always, always, always include a picture that will make people stop and read the post.

Tip #6 – Measure, Refine, Rinse & Repeat

The last thing that you need to do when you are creating and operating a FANtastic website is to measure the data. You cannot improve a website if you cannot measure its effectiveness. Measuring where your leads are coming from, what type of marketing is working and what pages are generating the most traffic is very important to fine-tuning your website success.

As I mentioned earlier, Google Analytics is an excellent tool for measuring the performance of your website. You can track data in so many ways. You can easily cross-reference where your real organic traffic is coming from versus where you are spending marketing dollars. After studying the information for a period of time, you will begin to see where your site does well and where it needs help.

We recommend you review the following Google Analytics (at a minimum) reports on a monthly basis:

- Audience Overview
- Acquisition>All Traffic>Source/Medium
- Behavior>Site Content>All Pages
- Behavior>Events>Overview
- Conversions>Goals>Overview

Make sure you have full administrative access to your Google Analytics account. Full access allows you to decide who can view and edit the reports instead of giving your webmaster that sole authority. If you forget to check your Google Analytics reports regularly, ask your webmaster to set up a recurring email report so the information is pushed into your inbox.

Creating and maintaining a FANtastic website is no longer an option for any business in any industry. A FANtastic website is a necessity for any company that wishes to be competitive in the information age.

The six steps listed above will guide you to create the right website for your home-building business. Engage the visitor and make them a fan, keep their attention by being visually stunning, place relevant information on your site which is easy to use and manage a blog that provides relevant and non-salesy language. From the back-end of your site, make sure you use a CMS which is easy to operate, update your site daily to make sure that content is fresh and accurate and always check your data so you can fine-tune your FANtastic site.

I wish for you nothing but unparalleled FANtastic success in your business. Don't hesitate to reach out if I can help you on your journey!

Mollie Elkman is a thought leader on marketing for the home building industry. She specializes in understanding the consumer experience and creating successful, traffic-driving advertising programs for builders from coast to coast. Mollie is an international speaker on all subjects relating to marketing for the building industry, with audiences ranging from small team training sessions to large conferences, including National Association of Home Builders, the International Builders Show, regional Home Builder Association conferences, the Pacific Coast Builders Conference, and NAHB 20 Clubs. Mollie's commitment to understanding the consumer experience and what motivates home buyers to action is widely known in the industry. She has an infectious passion for marketing new homes and is driven by the opportunity to help builders succeed. Prior to joining Group Two, Mollie learned the ins and outs of the advertising world at two leading creative agencies located in Florida and Southern California. She has worked on large and successful campaigns for companies within a variety of industries.

Marketing Matters

If you are reading this book then you already know you have something to learn about new home sales and marketing. The truth is, everyone does. Not only is our industry always evolving, but so are consumers. Therefore, the only way to really be an expert is to know you will NEVER be an expert. I have never written a full book on new home marketing because I'm sure by the time it is published, too much will have changed. As opportunities to reach buyers get deeper and deeper into digital strategies and tactics, it's becoming more complex to know where to start. So to make this as easy as possible…you should start right here, with the fundamentals of new home marketing which have been proven over time in our ever-changing industry and world.

Differentiation

Without a deep dive into who you are and who you are not, your marketing will never be great. Great marketing for any business starts from the top. The visionary. Most business owners, however, have a hard time simplifying their own message, which makes it impossible for the rest of the team to be the voice of that message. To make it easier, we have developed fun, interactive exercises to get your valuable vision down on paper. By doing this, you will start the process of taking your organization from just a company to a true brand with an identifiable and clear value. Here is a sample…

Company Differentiation Exercise

1. If your company was a car, what car would it be?
2. If you have to show a picture to represent your company, without showing a house, what would it be?
3. If your company were a famous person (living, dead or fictional) who would s/he be?

4. If the people at your company wore a uniform, what would it look like?

5. If your company had a theme song, what would it be?

Thinking about your brand from a different vantage point is an important part of the creative process. For example, if your homes were a car, what kind of car would they be? Ask this question to every person who works with you. You will be amazed at the responses you get. In one builder's feedback, we saw a full range of car brands, from a Ford truck to a Lexus. All good answers, given specifically to address the product and customer service. But ultimately, the builder was adamant their brand was aligned with Prius for their energy efficiency. This little exercise was a valuable start to a conversation that was clearly needed to identify their key differentiator.

There are only so many unique selling propositions out there, and every new home builder can't sell homes by saying the same thing. Your market, company, homes and service are different from every other builder out there. By trying to use a cookie-cutter approach to sales and marketing, you are actually diluting your efforts and missing the opportunity to show buyers why they should build with YOU. Every builder has SOMETHING to say about Price, Product, Location, Customer Service and the Experience they have. But when you have the ONE thing that sets you apart in your market, you can really start to tell a unique story which will connect with buyers on a deeper level.

By evaluating these differentiation exercises and doing market and competitive analyses, we are able to identify a position in the market only you can own. When you truly own that message on every level, you will differentiate yourself from all other options out there. If something is different, buyers want to see it. This approach makes consumers visit you online and on-site prior to making any purchasing decisions. After all, that is the ultimate goal with marketing--getting the right prospects in the door so your sales team can sell homes.

Mood

Now that you know what you stand for, you need to visually bring it to life. What colors, textures and images align with your brand? A mood board is an extremely valuable tool for your overall marketing. When done correctly, a strong mood board will evoke the feelings you want people to have when they interact with your company at every step of the home buying process. It's an amazing example of how simple images can say so much. For mood board samples, check out
MarketingMatters.GroupTwo.com

Voice

Of course, the visuals need to match the tone of voice of your message. No matter where you are putting your message, content will always be a fundamental of great marketing. Most builders default to using industry terms and information-driven messaging. That's not necessarily wrong for certain audiences, but most consumers need to FEEL something in order to interact with and respond to your brand. Rather than telling them who you are, you want to show them how you make their lives better by painting a picture with words. Is your tone fun and playful? Is it professional and direct? Remember, you don't need a "serious" tone to be taken seriously. A warm and conversational tone of voice can be perfect for a first-time home buyer who is young and new to the experience. A witty and laid-back tone might be perfect for a 55+ community that offers a fun, relaxed lifestyle. No matter what tone of voice represents your company and team, the key objective with your content is to earn trust.

Brand Guide

One way to earn trust is by having a clear, consistent, recognizable brand. When your marketing is consistent, buyers start to feel like they know you. Every time someone interacts with your company--from social media, to your website, to your points of sale--they are trusting you more and more. No matter what your starting price is, to your buyers, this is the largest purchase of their lives. If your marketing looks disorganized, or like it was done on the side by the owner's nephew who is still finishing school, your buyers will sense it. They will question where else you cut corners. And you will miss out on making a very important connection--and building a sense of trust--at the very start of the process. For a brand guide sample, visit **MarketingMatters.GroupTwo.com**

Creative

Once you have a brand guide, it's important that you follow it. This is one part of the marketing plan many building companies have a hard time with. I hear "Oh, we follow it internally, but our sign guys don't need to because they just do their own thing." Ummmm, no. This is YOUR brand and it's representative of your relationship with your buyers. Every single touch point needs to earn their trust, including your signage. You can have many different campaigns throughout the year, but they should still follow your brand guide. You can create event invites, spec sheets and homeowner handbooks that all accomplish a unique goal, while still representing the brand image. Want to see some inspiring creative? Check out some of our favorites here **MarketingMatters.GroupTwo.com**

Media

Now that you know what to say and what visuals to show, it's time to determine where to say it. This is the part that changes for each of you in your specific markets. I can tell you with 100% certainty that anyone who says print is dead does not work in all markets across the U.S., with all buyer demographics. The same with billboards. I can also tell you digital is essential in every market. It usually makes sense for a good portion of your marketing dollars to be allocated to digital marketing which will provide a very trackable and real return on your investment. Your company is not the same as anyone else's, so don't ever expect your marketing strategy to be, either. Want to see a media strategy sample? Visit **MarketingMatters.GroupTwo.com**

Results

This is the point of this entire book. You may think your marketing is just fine, but if it isn't sending the right buyers to your door so you can ultimately sell homes and meet goals then it's just a pretty image and a fun headline. Truly great marketing is all about results. Getting people to stop and listen. Getting them to act--to call, to go to the website, to come into a sales center. The best part of marketing today is that it is easier to track than ever before. In order to track what you are doing, though, you need to have a basic understanding of marketing. It's important to ask questions of those you trust with your brand. It's also okay to explore new tactics. Just don't blindly do something because the builder down the street is. When it comes to results, marketing matters. And one size doesn't fit all.

Take a moment...
Do you know the one thing which makes you different?
Are you earning trust with your marketing efforts?
Are you tracking results in real time?

Will Duderstadt is currently the VP of Digital Marketing at M/I Homes, Inc., one of the nation's leading builders of single-family homes, having delivered over 100,000 homes. Will oversees online marketing campaigns, lead generation, SEO, PPC, Social Media and content strategy for 16 divisions in 11 states. Will provides insight and leadership for M/I Homes' Internet Sales Manager program and Marketing Managers, training the team in best practices for lead-creation and management.

- Selected to Professional Builder's 40 Under 40 in 2017

- Joined the Zillow Group (ZG) New Home Builder Advisory Board in 2016

- Awarded Corporate Excellence Award at M/I Homes in 2013

- 4 time speaker at NAHB International Builder Show (2018, 2017, 2016, 2015)

Previously, Will was a founding partner of MCLA The Lax Mag, a print magazine covering college lacrosse, which was acquired by Inside Lacrosse (an ESPN affiliate) in December 2011. Will also served in various positions at Apple Inc. (AAPL) for five years and was featured as a spotlight speaker on apple.com.

Online Sales is Just Sales

How Did We Get Here?

Fifteen short years ago, shopping for a home was a completely different experience. If we could travel back to 2003 for a quick visit, we would barely recognize the shopping and buying process, much less how the real estate industry was using technology. The bestselling mobile phone that year was a Nokia 1100, popular because it had a color screen. The first iPhone was still four years away. YouTube and Facebook were just glints in the eyes of their creators. And as archaic as it might be to us now, the most up-to-date way a consumer could browse real estate listings was probably in the Sunday newspaper. The motivated buyer would endlessly drive neighborhoods looking for yard signs, while the savviest might get their hands on the coveted MLS book, printed just once a week for MLS members. The transition from shopping to buying was blurred, as often both took place in our sales offices, requiring hours upon hours of walking homesites, reviewing floorplans and discussing options and colors. Consumers arrived not ready to buy, but full of questions and seeking information. My friend Dennis O'Neil articulates this interaction between buyer and salesperson best in his book <u>Sales Actualization: Outselling the Internet</u>. *"Before the Internet, we were the gatekeepers of information. We controlled the data and you were forced to speak to one of us to get even the most basic answers."* As a gatekeeper, a salesperson had perceived value. They controlled the flow of critical information like lot availability, price and community milestone dates. Eventually, our consumers would be armed with brochures and folders from dozens of builders. They retreated to their dining room tables to spread out. Families would gather around to compare Builder A to Builder B, some only memorable for the weight and gloss of the paper their plans were printed on. Meanwhile, our sales teams leveraged a key piece of cutting-edge technology--the telephone--following up relentlessly with the only communication methods available. Building relationships, taking introductions and providing updates on price changes and new communities. To excel in sales was to build valuable, meaningful relationships, to deliver solutions to solve client's needs, and to provide value during a significant and often confusing purchase process.

Somewhere along the way, things changed. Technology allowed for the organization and mass distribution of information. When Zillow launched in 2006 on a mission to *build the largest, most trusted, and vibrant home-related marketplace in the world*, they had an audience of consumers hungry for greater visibility into homes for sale, home prices and economic trends in housing--information which was previously available only through a salesperson. But now it's needed on-demand. In fact, with America's desire to understand how home values were so strong, Zillow logged over one-million visitors in the first three days of their website going live. The site itself actually crashed within the first few hours. Meanwhile, Google had spent years *organizing the world's information*. They were established in our minds as the friendly librarian who helped navigate an enormous online library. Millions of users started their Internet journey on Google's simple, utilitarian homepage, relying on them to bring order to the chaos of the Internet. As a user, you knew you wanted to *shop for cars* or *see scores from the Cubs game*. Which website Google took you to was less important than answering your query. Few sites had built enough of a brand or reputation to become a destination site. The expectation had been set that you could find anything in Google.

In hindsight, organizing the knowledge and data on every home in America seems obvious to us. After all, information wants to be free--at least that's Stewart Brand's opinion. As founder of the Whole Earth Catalog, a publication Steve Jobs would famously liken to "Google in paperback format," Brand led a counterculture movement which embraced self-sufficiency and a *do-it-yourself* attitude. The right information at the right time has the profound ability to shape and improve our lives, free not in price, but freedom for all to access and containing the transparency to understand the information. Information will always have value and costs associated with distributing it. As the Internet has shown us, information cannot be caged. The progress technology provided us is remarkably simple in theory (though wildly difficult in execution). Just as Stewart Brand had, they understood the power of information. Companies like Zillow and Google have opened the cage door and allowed information to fly free. They distributed that information in an easy-to-use interface, more akin to Facebook than an IRS tax form.

Back in 2003, brands across all industries built new and engaging websites, knowing they had to be findable on Google. This was also the early days of SEO (Search Engine Optimization), or the idea of modifying your website to be better positioned in search results. Now it's 2018. Much like then, real estate professionals across the country understand their listings need to be discoverable anywhere a consumer decides to browse.

But we're on the cusp of a new era, where it's no longer enough to just be there--whether that's Facebook, Zillow or our own website. Our communities, plans and listings need to rise above the rest. Publishing literal content for our product isn't enough. Customers crave more! Done right, content tells a story. It builds an emotional bond between builder and prospect. In a 2015 Economist article, (https://www.fjordnet.com/conversations/liquid-expectations/) Baiju Shah coined the phrase *Liquid Expectations*. Simply put, it's the concept that when consumers interact with one product or company, their point of view on other (often unrelated) products and services shifts the expectations of an experience flowing from interaction with one company to interaction with the next. This can include the world class customer service of Nordstrom, the ease of ordering online with Amazon or the personalized service of your local Starbucks barista. Aware of the driving force or not, modern marketers are being forced to look beyond direct competition and evaluate the experiences being delivered outside their core industry. The standards are being raised, and I suspect many builders are not ready. The popular e-commerce site Zappos is a prime example of Liquid Expectations for publishing content. For every product being sold, they build out a robust library of content to help the customer understand their product. That's 20+ photographs, nearly 90 seconds of videos, and dozens of reviews from loyal customers for a single pair of shoes. Take a look at your product online. Does it deliver the same message and detail? The ride-sharing phenomenon Uber facilitates over two-million rides per day. Riding Uber is easy. Launch the app, click a button and a clean car with a personal driver is dispatched. Within five minutes, an Uber ride appears at your location, ready to whisk you away to your destination. Comparatively, are you disappointing customers with slow follow-up or slow service? Today, letting a single call go to voicemail is enough to lose a sale. If you are a regular coffee drinker like me, your local Starbucks barista might remember you when you walk through the door. They will probably call you by name and often will start preparing your favorite drink. This personalization of services is not unlike the homepage of Amazon.com, which displays recently-viewed and recommended products. Does your sales team personalize the buying experience?

Complete and engaging content is a requirement. Those who go above and beyond, embracing full online transparency, will stand out. Any sales pitches or USPs that would have been uttered in a sales office back in 2003 are now ripe to become online content-- transparency not only on *what* we are selling, but *how* we sell it-- our builder story, our happy homeowners and our construction process. You will still wow your customers with state-of-the-art construction methods, luxurious amenities and innovative designs. In 2018, make sure you are sharing that story online and not just in your sales offices.

Time for a Change.

So now that every detail of what and how we build is published online, what's the role of sales? The distinction between shopping and buying has never been clearer. Instead of a dining room table, families gather around the warm glow of an iPad in the living room. They quickly send listings to each other via their mobile devices. Tidbits of information are gathered as consumers stand in line at the grocery store. I wouldn't be surprised if people are favoriting homes as they sit at red lights. It's that easy to shop. And as that ease of browsing increases, making the leap to buying becomes harder. Analysis paralysis can keep a well-intentioned consumer in the shopping process longer than they intended. There's that nagging voice in their head telling them to keep shopping. "There's always one more home to see, to wait for a deal." "Prices might drop next month," or they may even talk themselves out of buying altogether. "Building new takes too long."

This is where our Online Sales Consultants enter! A skilled OSC becomes a guide rather than a gatekeeper, expertly navigating the shopping and buying process--the trusted friend who can provide advice and a concierge to make our customers' lives easier.

You might look at your organization and think, "I have a great salesperson onsite. I'll let them fill that role." OSCs live in a world vastly different from our traditional onsite salespeople. They take communication to the next level, being masters of all channels-- telephone, of course, but also email, SMS, social media and video. They listen far more than they talk. They empower consumers to take the next step. Done successfully, they motivate the transition from online to real life.

A builder considering adding an OSC to their staff should assess their business on a few factors. First, are you generating demand for your product in the form of inbound calls or electronic leads, or do you have a deep backlog of leads who need to be contacted? Your OSC can only be successful if a good marketing plan is in place to drive viable leads to them, consistently over time. Resist the urge to task your OSC with electronic marketing, as well. As a builder of any size, it is difficult, if not impossible, to effectively manage both. But do ensure your Marketing Manager (or agency) and your OSC are best friends. They will need to rely on each other. Second, are you equipped to accept an influx of appointments in your sales office? Most builders will jump at the chance to increase traffic to their sales offices. Take a critical look at the capacity of your onsite sales team. They will need to prepare for scheduled meetings every day of the week. Their use of an electronic calendar is non-negotiable. Finally, how many incremental sales can you realistically add without disrupting your construction process? This will drive both your marketing efforts--aka how many leads you should plan to generate in a particular month--as well as the goals for your OSC.

Once you've identified the need and have begun the search to grow your team, you'll need a skilled OSC to focus on three key factors. Pure speed is the first, foremost and most critical trait they'll need to possess. All inbound phone calls need to be answered immediately. Email leads with phone numbers should be called back within minutes. Text messages, social media inquiries, website chat requests, and any other notification of interest from a consumer need real-time responses. This means your OSCs should be fully-dedicated to the task at hand, with little to no additional work functions competing for their attention. Second is an undying commitment to delivering the highest customer service possible. Manners and politeness are free and should be given to your customers in excess. Be gracious, kind and welcoming. Listen to every word your customer has to say. Third, know the goal and stay focused. OSCs have a singular goal. It's not to sell a home or to capture a deposit. It is to drive highly-qualified appointments to your on-site sales team. An OSC who remains singularly-focused on this task will become a rich source of business for your communities and you will always be in a position to gauge their performance.

The More Things Change, the More They Stay the Same.

Think of a recent party or networking event you might have attended. Imagine a friendly stranger approaching you with an outstretched hand introducing himself. "Hi there! I'm on sale today at a 10% discount for new clients," he says. "Would you like to see a demonstration of my product?" This is not a successful or engaging first impression. Instead, think of how this really happens. Two strangers talk about the weather, the event they are attending--or perhaps they share a mutual friend. Rapport is built as compliments are traded and jokes are told. A great conversation is fluid, with each person reacting to the other, moving the dialog forward. Receiving leads generated from your website is just like meeting someone at this party. Your OSCs will invest time and energy into their new leads and build meaningful relationships. With their knowledge of all your communities, they are uniquely equipped to deliver the best recommendation to solve their client's needs. They can artfully explain the process of building a new home and dispel any fears. Eventually, the successful OSC will drive this highly-qualified, ready, willing and able buyer into your sales office.

As you can see, it's only the tools that are different. Just as it was fifteen years ago, it will be fifteen years in the future. As such, the old adage holds true. *The more things change, the more they stay the same.* To excel in online sales is to build valuable, meaningful relationships, to deliver solutions to solve clients' needs and to provide value during a significant and often confusing purchase process.

Angela McKay is the Vice President, Client Experience at Lasso Data Systems, the leading CRM for home builders and developers. With Lasso for over 10 years, Angela has consulted and helped clients by providing online strategy and email marketing expertise to help homebuilders achieve better results. Angela is also actively involved in NAHB's PWB Council and is the former Communication and Education Chair. She has a tendency to roll up her sleeves and get involved in all aspects of her life. To say she manages a full plate is probably an understatement but she thrives on a challenging workload and prefers the words "intentionally full" to busy!

Culture Shift: Embracing Change

Technology is a given in the world of sales, and technology is evolving faster than many of us can adapt. The way things were done as short as two-to-three years ago is different from today. Workflow evolves, as do the methods in which we communicate and access information. Salespeople need to be nimble, open-minded and adaptable, and yet these are not always the top traits of high-performing sales professionals. It's easy to tell people to embrace change, but for most, especially salespeople, it can be difficult.

As humans, we are, for the most part, open-minded, but we also crave the familiar. We take comfort in the predictable and the routine. It's hard to break out of a secure routine. Often, the older we get, the harder it becomes. We need to get better at adapting to change as it can hinder our growth potential and the value we provide to our employer.

Why do some sales people dislike CRM so much? The truth of the matter is most salespeople prefer talking and interacting with people rather than entering information into a CRM system. There is no denying the fact that some salespeople view CRM as a means for their manager to keep tabs on them. There is an obvious correlation between sales activity and the number of sales made, so getting bogged down entering information and updating records may appear tedious and unproductive. What isn't readily realized by salespeople are all the lost, forgotten prospects.

Change can be disruptive and cause some discomfort, so when a new technology (like CRM) is introduced, salespeople may resist.

How do you get your sales reps to buy into CRM?

1. **Team Awareness of the CRM**
   Involve the team in the process--whether it's including representatives from the sales team on the selection group or providing regular updates and information to the entire sales team during the learning process. Ensure they have a thorough understanding of pending changes. It's natural to be more receptive to new systems and changes when everyone feels they are a part of the solution.

2. **Establish Measurable Goals**
   This sounds so simple, but it's often overlooked. Goals refer to both the simple and more complex. A simple goal might include, *By the end of this year, everyone should be logging into the CRM and updating prospects.* A more complex (but still very-much achievable) goal might be, *Everyone should establish full visibility into our best lead sources, increase Lead to Appointment conversions by 25% and increase Appointment to Purchase by 30%.* Write out your goals, team goals and company goals. Create work-back tasks to keep everyone on track and provide regular check-ins.

3. **Your Culture**
   The most successful companies are focused on customer experience. Sales and profit will naturally follow. According to **Gartner Research,** *over 89% of companies feel they compete mostly on the basis of customer experience,* and according to **Gallup News' State of American Workplace** research we learn that *happy employees mean a 20% higher chance your buyers will also be happy.* A happier employee is more productive, and they ultimately provide a better experience to buyers as they are far more likely to embrace successful processes. Your entire organization--this includes sales, admin, marketing and project managers--need to all understand your priorities. Once you have a common vision, you can then relate back to the purpose of systems. A well-known quote from Steve Jobs rings true. *"You've got to start with the customer experience and work back*

toward the technology, not the other way around."

4. **Start Slowly**

   If you start off with technology which is too sophisticated, it has a negative effect on team adoption. If your team is new to a structured sales process, keep it simple and allow it to evolve as the reps become more comfortable and familiar with the system. Remember to get their input along the way. Ensure everyone knows where to go for help and when they seek help, it should always be given in a positive manner.

5. **Training**

   Many times, companies rely only on the CRM company to provide training on the new system. However, training should also take place internally, outlining processes and clear definitions of leads. Something as simple as *How to Enter a Prospect* should be clearly understood by everyone on your team. Your CRM provider will provide the *how-to* training, but you need to provide the *why* training.

   Training needs to be ongoing. The size of your organization will determine the frequency and approach, whether it's a regular item at your sales meetings or dedicated sessions scheduled throughout the year. Technology training should be included in every employee's professional development plan.

   We've all been to events where we learn new things and are excited and motivated to put them into practice. Then we get back to the office and revert right back to the way things were before. Why? Because most of us aren't disciplined enough to take on initiatives on our own. We don't plan. Having a sales coach to mentor and help sales agents can contribute significantly to the company's overall success.

6. **Apply Knowledge to the Day-to-Day Problems**

Help your team understand the value of the data to the company. Extraordinary data can be extracted to determine the approach to sales, such as where the best sources of leads are as well as the demographics of buyers. Ensure your team knows how to find their most enthusiastic prospects and have the ability to review a prospect before they come in for an appointment. Show them the benefits of detail building in the prospect profile. Provide continual reinforcement and discussion to ensure good habits are formed.

7. **Proper Set Up**
   Everyone's in a rush! While every CRM company should have the best interests of their clients in mind and will always want to ensure that you are set up and seeing value as quickly as possible, trying to push it too fast can make your users suffer. Allow time to fully communicate how the CRM is going to benefit and help your sales team. For example, review your ratings with your team prior to implementing the CRM and ensure everyone is on the same page as to when and how you use them. Always make sure your team can begin using the software right after they are trained. The adage *use it or lose it* holds true in this case.

How Can You Improve Usage?

CRM is a bit like a sales assistant for a sales rep--it keeps them organized, manages their activities and appointments and helps them accomplish more in less time. Ultimately, this means more deals closed and increased revenue for your company and your team.

1. **Model by Example**
   Managers will play a key role in CRM adoption throughout the organization. The purpose of the CRM is to coach your team to a higher level of performance. Managers show the way by being actively involved and utilizing the system themselves.

2. **Ask for Input/Be Open to Feedback**
You need the sales team to enter data into the CRM, otherwise the data becomes useless. Listen to the salespeople's feedback and concerns and act on them when appropriate to encourage company-wide adoption. Your CRM provider should help you by identifying areas in the software that will be most beneficial to your team.

3. **Celebrate Wins**
By demonstrating value, you will be demonstrating the ROI of the system. A more efficient organization of the data may make it easier for the salesperson at the model homes to truly understand who is interested in each phase of the building.

Providing a great experience for the buyer requires a systematic approach to selling. We know this can be a challenge for salespeople. They often sell naturally, and in most cases, correctly, as they inherently know what needs to be done to close a sale. However, sales can fall through the cracks when you don't have a proper process in place. Business is evolving and buyers are changing. In order to remain competitive, we need to be progressive and think differently. Making these changes can be difficult, but with a common-sense approach, what may originally feel like a chore will eventually become routine.

Take a Moment...

Let me tell you a story about change and what you can achieve with proper planning. While it has nothing to do with sales, the parallels are significant. Last year, I got the crazy idea that I wanted to run a marathon. I have always been a runner--not fast, just slow and steady. Having participated in many 10k runs and half marathons, I thought it was time to go for the full marathon. Running 26.2 miles seemed unfathomable, but millions of people do it. By creating a plan, I figured I could, as well. I learned two things in the process. First, when you make something a priority, you get it done, and second, when you create a plan and stick to it, you achieve your goal.

I equipped myself with the necessary tools (proper shoes, a training program and fitness tracking devices and apps) and I followed the prescribed plan to a T (sometimes running at 5am or 10pm to ensure I got my run in.) I developed habits, made sacrifices and ran the marathon in a better time than I had hoped.

The exact same approach can apply to sales--prioritize, plan and execute. When you apply this to business, you move forward and gain in accomplishments. Training is doing your homework. It may not be the most exciting part of your work, but if you stick with it over time, you will see incremental improvements. Work will get easier, more routine and natural--and you'll see results. Not all positive changes feel positive in the beginning. Training for the marathon had its share of ups and downs and required some pivoting, but surpassing my goal was worth the discomfort.

THIS PAGE IS INTENTIONALLY BLANK

Alaina Money, aka Buildlikeagirl is a homebuilder, writer and mom to three rowdy feminists in progress, and one tiny misbehaving dog. Alaina is founder and CEO of Garman Homes and Fresh Paint by Garman Homes. Prior to her current role, Alaina was employee #3 at Garman Homes and managed both the sales and construction teams before serving as Division President. She documents every success and failure of her career in her award winning blog, Build Like a Girl. Alaina was named to Professional Builder's list of 40 Under 40 for the class of 2015. Alaina has also been named Builder of the Year twice - in 2015 by the HBA of Durham Orange County and in 2017 by the HBA of Raleigh-Wake. Alaina is currently focusing all of her professional energy on a national expansion strategy for Fresh Paint by Garman Homes. She and her partner, Jim Garman will be opening Fresh Paint - Denver in 2020.

Becoming a Meaningfully Different Homebuilder

In 2007, Jim Garman met the Executive Officer of his local Home Builders Association and told him he wanted to start his own homebuilding company. The response wasn't what Jim was expecting. Initially, the Executive Officer tried to talk him out of it. Realizing Jim's mind was made up, he asked one simple question. "What makes you different?" He warned, "You've got to know the answer to that question."

About a year after that conversation, I called Jim and told him I wanted to start his sales team at Garman Homes. He and I had met earlier in the day and had walked one of his homes together, but at the end of our meeting, he didn't offer me a job. So I decided to call him up and ask for one. Jim and I knew each other briefly from our days working together at a large national builder. I was onsite sales and Jim was, as I referred to him then, the 12-year old running construction and operations.

At the time when I called Jim and offered myself a job, I was a very successful salesperson for a different national homebuilder. That year I was nominated for and won the MAME Award for Salesperson of the Year. I could have worked for almost any builder in our area. I chose to work for Garman Homes. In fact, I was desperate to work for Garman Homes because it was *different*.

Jim sold and closed twelve houses his first year of operation. My very first month selling Garman Homes, I sold eleven. To say the least, I was inspired. And now, more than eleven years later, I still wake up inspired. I'm thrilled to work for Garman Homes and proud beyond measure to now serve as its CEO.

Jim took the advice of his local HBA Executive Officer and started Garman Homes with Four Garman Differences.

#1 *Rock Stars* Wanted

We hire people with superior attitudes who wake up every morning to offer a great homebuilding experience. *Rock Stars* want to put on a show! They enjoy what they do and they love delighting the people around them.

#2 Guaranteed Closing Date

That's right! When you sign a purchase agreement on a Garman Home, you get a Guaranteed Closing Date. If we miss it, we offer $1000 in additional closing costs.

#3 The G Team

Our warranty team shows up at 45 days and 11 months after you close on your new Garman Home. A select group of trades who helped build your new home show up after you move in to inspect their own work as well as address any warrantable items.

#4 Give it Back

For every home we sell, a portion of the sale goes towards local causes and charities. When you purchase a Garman Home, your purchase gives back to your local community.

On the surface, these Four Garman Differences are demonstrable, observable and even measurable ways potential buyers can differentiate our homebuilding company from the next. It is the answer to the question, "What makes you different?"

Beneath the surface, however, these same Four Garman Differences became our internal organizational compass. They were the foundational elements we would use to grow our company in a meaningfully different way. Each of these Four Garman Differences offers a deeper dive into what it takes behind the scenes to deliver on the promise of a great homebuilding experience.

Rock Stars Wanted = CULTURE

The culture of your company, whether intentional, evolving or circumstantial, will set the tone of your builder identity. Every person on your team is a reflection of your company. If you're the owner, that means every person on your team is a reflection of YOU. This last sentence either made you happy, made you ponder a bit or made you outright cringe. That's okay. We've all been there. Culture requires constant maintenance, but when you get it right, it sets the team on fire.

For us, being a *Rock Star* isn't just about offering the *buyer* a great experience; it's about searching for ways to elevate the homebuilding experience for anyone and everyone we meet. It's about the way we treat our trade partners, developer partners, cooperating brokers and EACH OTHER.

Our culture, and more importantly our chemistry with one another, are our single biggest assets. We hire people with superior attitudes. It's easy to have a great attitude when everything is going well, but what about when it's not? Can you still keep up the positivity? Or what about maintaining the commitment to elevating the experience for everyone when someone is screaming at you in an ALL CAPS email? It's not as easy as it sounds!

It's the small things we do, like the way we start an email by asking how someone is doing, or remembering a small detail about their personal lives before launching in to a list of demands or inquiries. It's remembering the names of the people who work at the Town and asking them how we can become their favorite builder. It may sound silly, but trust me...it works. They will tell you!

It's also the big things like referring an unrepresented buyer to a cooperating broker we know and trust because we understand the buyer would benefit from their guidance, or when we design a new product for our developer partners to help them, and us, reach a new market segment.

Being a *Rock Star* is an unapologetically high bar. The only way we can meet or exceed our own expectations is by filling each other up with positivity. We do this by giving each other the benefit of the doubt, inviting people to bring their whole selves to work and reassuring them they will be accepted and loved exactly as they are. (Unless who they are is miserable and grumpy, in which case, they probably wouldn't have been hired.) It is everyone's responsibility to uphold, defend and protect the culture. That's what keeps *Rock Stars* performing at such a high level.

We fire people for having bad attitudes. We've paid dearly when we've allowed someone to stay who cannot live up to the *Rock Stars Wanted* promise. More often than not the person being let go is shocked, unaware their attitude had changed dramatically. Sometimes it is nothing more than the difference between being on auto-pilot and waking up every morning with intention. We're not looking for auto-pilots. *Rock Stardom* requires vigilance.

Rock Stardom is never a given. It is a title that must be earned, every day in new and different ways. Our culture is the space we create for each other to stay inspired and do our best work together.

What your culture conveys is important. Make sure it's the message you want to be sending.

Guaranteed Closing Date = OPERATIONAL EXCELLENCE

I'm not big on sports analogies but I love the grainy images of Babe Ruth stepping up to the plate and pointing his bat to left center field in an attempt to put the stadium on notice that he was about to do something BIG.

Every time we give a buyer a Guaranteed Closing Date, we're stepping up to the plate and pointing our proverbial bats [bulldozers, hard hats, hammers...] toward left center field. We are putting everyone on notice that no matter the time of year, the ease or difficulty of the plan, the type of loan or the scarcity of supplies, we are going to close this home on this date! We even offer a wager. We give the buyer $1000 if we miss it.

Have we missed one? Yes! We've missed more than I'd like to admit. Still, in nearly a dozen years of homebuilding, our batting average is hovering in the mid-.900's. That's way better than Babe. No offense to The Great Bambino.

We think everyone performs better with a deadline--the buyer, the trades and especially, construction managers.

When the buyer has a Guaranteed Closing Date, it eliminates the stress and uncertainty of a 30-60 day closing window and allows them to focus on all the things they need to do in order to purchase their new home on time--price their home to sell quickly, get their loan approvals in order, sign off on selections on time, schedule movers, register for schools, etc. The list of what the buyer has to do to finalize the purchase of their new home is almost as extraordinary as is the list to build their home.

We learned from our trade partners that if we were going to offer a Guaranteed Closing Date, we'd better get our processes in order. We dug in with our trade partners to understand how our process could reflect exactly what they needed in order to be successful and hit our Guaranteed Dates. It was actually pretty basic.

They needed to know WHAT they were building [*accurate plans, completed job starts,*] HOW to build it [*selection sheets with detailed diagrams and frequent face time with the construction managers.*] They needed to RECEIVE purchase orders that matched the work they did [*for the price we've already agreed upon*] and be PAID quickly [*in dollars, not hugs.*] Not specifically asked for but also vital is treating them with respect and gratitude for the work they do. And as a rule, we always say please and thank you.

For a construction manager, having a Guaranteed Closing Date is the difference between throwing their hands in the air when something is delayed or making 5-10 extra phone calls to figure out a solution to overcome the delay. It's walking every house, every room, every day. Period. It's managing construction in real time, not batching calls to make or documents to send at some future point. Great construction managers know what's happening on all their jobsites at all times. They know who is supposed to show up when, and if they don't, they know why and how to get them there ASAP.

It's not easy, but a Guaranteed Closing Date sends a message to everyone that you aren't afraid to do something BIG. You are the expert. Don't be afraid to bet on yourself and your team. You can either do the best you can, or you can set a deadline and move hell and high water to hit it. It's up to you.

The G Team = BUILD THE RELATIONSHIP FIRST

Offering a great homebuilding experience includes showing up still as committed to the cause after the buyers move in to their new home as before. Warranty work has a very low bar in our industry for a variety of reasons. Some buyers don't understand the regular maintenance of their new home, some buyers expect the builder to take care of everything [*I was once called to change a fluorescent tube in the pantry*] and some builders--true to the stereotype many homeowners fear--are just not as responsive after the homeowner moves in.

I get it. Warranty work can be a sticky situation ripe with disappointments for both parties. We don't have it all figured out. We still occasionally get the 1-star review-slash-rant on Facebook. It destroys me for a minute until I realize there's a lesson to be learned somewhere in that rant. The buyer is stressed. We're trying to set boundaries. It can be tense. Still, this is an area where all builders can differentiate their experience. The work starts well before the buyer moves in.

One of the sayings I'm known for repeating over and over is, "Build the Relationship first." We even have it printed on a huge sign in our Design Studio--strategically placed behind where the buyer sits and facing our team. It's a reminder that the quality of the relationships we build will determine the quality of the homebuilding and warranty experience for everyone.

Some of the ways we build the relationship include an introductory email congratulating the buyer on going under contract. The salesperson tells us a little about the buyers, what they're building and why this home is so special to them. This allows the team to respond in thoughtful ways to begin building the relationship with the buyer. Then later, when the buyer is in the Design Studio, the team welcomes them like someone they already know. The buyer is at ease after being introduced to more members of the team.

Once the home is under construction, during pre-construction and pre-drywall meetings, construction managers are encouraged to tell the buyers about some of the people who will be constructing their new home. Using their names and not just *the framer* or *the masons*--we tell them about our crews and why we're proud to have each and every one of them on our jobsites. All of this builds trust and a foundational relationship which can sustain the ups and downs that occur during construction.

One more important tip about building the relationship. Insist members of your team refer to buyers by their names instead of their lot numbers or floorplans. Sounds obvious, right? And yet, how many times have you heard someone say, "Lot 150 called and they want to know when that broken window will be replaced?" If you want to build a genuine relationship with buyers, insist that your team refer to them by their names first and identifying details second. "Hey, Jim and Alaina called this morning. They're building the Castle in Brooklyn with that gorgeous custom island on Lot 150. They wanted to see when the broken window will be replaced."

Small changes make a big difference. Build the relationship first.

Give It Back – HOW A HOMEBUILDING COMPANY CAN CHANGE THE WORLD

Every home we build gives back to a local cause. Over the years we've given back in all sorts of ways.

We regularly donate to Habitat for Humanity of Durham, NC.

This past summer we completed our 9th Builder's Blitz home where we constructed a home from foundation to finish in six days. There's something poetic about our homeowners paying it forward and making it possible for other people to reach their dream of homeownership.

In 2015 we built The Miracle Home for the MIX 101.5 Radiothon to support Duke Children's Hospital. We donated $200K. The Miracle Home is still my favorite home we've ever built and not just because we got to build a secret room. I'll never forget the joy on people's faces when they discovered this playroom, complete with swings, a stage, and built-in bookcases. It was pure magic! The Miracle Home is my favorite because the buyers who purchased this home had no idea it was The Miracle Home. They just loved the house. Upon learning of their home's legacy, the buyers broke down in tears. Both of their children were born prematurely. Were it not for places like Duke Children's Hospital, their babies might not have survived. Talk about a magical moment.

In 2017 we built Hero Home #16 for Operation Coming Home, an organization that gives homes to severely-wounded Veterans. We built the first home for a female recipient and the first home to honor a fallen soldier. We also made this the first Hero Home built by a female construction manager at a company led by a female Division President and owned, in part, by a woman. The spirit of giving back has never felt so powerful as it did in that moment.

Every opportunity we have to give back is an opportunity to live our mission--to be the builder we've always wanted to be. No matter how big or how small, giving back is how we all, as homebuilders, get the chance to be a homebuilding company that changes the world.

Key Thought:

As a builder, you must know who you are, who you aren't and

what makes you different. Once you find that out, work diligently to ensure that every part of your business reflects your identity.

Five Tips:

1.) Culture is your single biggest asset. Make sure it's the one you want.
2.) Set expectations high and hold people accountable. Fire people who don't make the cut.
3.) Everyone works better with a deadline.
4.) Build the relationship with your customers first. The quality of your relationship with your customer is commensurate with the quality of the experience for all involved.
5.) Always look for ways to give back.

As Vice President of Hubbell Homes, **Rachel Flint** provides strategic leadership, planning and oversight of the home building operations in Iowa and Florida. She leads all planning, development and implementation for the division, including construction, warranty, design, estimating and sales. Rachel joined Hubbell Realty Company in 2004, and has served in leadership roles for Hubbell's public relations, marketing and sales.

Rachel received a Bachelor of Arts degree from the University of Northern Iowa and a Master's degree in Communication Leadership from Drake University. She is a Certified Marketing Professional and Certified Sales Professional with the National Association of Home Builders. Rachel is currently a National Director for the NAHB, and is 2nd Vice President of the Greater Des Moines Home Builder's Association.

Know Your Numbers

I believe the only way to improve as a team is to first measure where you are--in everything. Whether you are a salesperson, a customer care specialist, a superintendent or the company owner, numbers should be the universal language spoken by all. One person in one sector of home building isn't going to get the job done alone. Once you *know* where you are, you can continue to where you *want* to be.

As Brian Tracy describes in his book *Flight Plan*, airline pilots do this every day. They take off from a certain location with a definite end destination. Since pilots know where they are at any given time in the air, they can adjust their course based on the varied conditions they may encounter. If they hit a rough patch of turbulence, they move higher to get above the bumps. Storms may cause the pilot to fly out of the way, adding time to the overall flight, or a nice jet stream may give an added boost to reduce flight time. In the end, almost every flight arrives safely at its desired location.

As homebuilders, we, too, should be cognizant of where we are and where we're headed. There will be turbulence encountered along the way--rising interest rates and hard costs, shortages of labor and growing competition. Like a pilot, we need to adjust, but as I tell our team, we are our own greatest threat. Four years ago, Hubbell Homes closed 179 homes. Today, we close well over 250 in 35 communities. This growth was only made possible by knowing our numbers, focusing on our strengths and bolstering our weaknesses.

As a production home builder in Des Moines, Iowa, there is a lot of competition. More than 350 homebuilders compete for buyers in a 650,000 Metropolitan Statistical Area (MSA) which produces roughly 3,200 building permits. Banks are generously loaning money, and to be a builder, one only needs a cell phone and a tablet. This adds to the competition.

Our market is a *spec-heavy* market, meaning there are fewer presold homes than speculative home sales. It is also a market dominated by Realtors. Rarely do builders have in-house sales teams, and 5–6% commission structures to outside agencies are the norm. Builders have tried the in-house route as encouraged by every other builder in America, but each has abandoned the strategy after experiencing a steep decline in sales. Selling a *spec*, or showcase home, means a payday within 60 days for a Realtor, whereas a presold means the check may not come for five months or more. Face the facts--presold homes are not as labor intensive as the showcase home sale.

With all this competition, I tell our team to focus on our numbers, not on those of the competition. Are we perfect? No. Nor is anyone else. We do, however, know where we are at any given time of the year so we can chart a course for our year-end destination. If we don't focus on our numbers, slippage may occur. As many business coaches have said, "Casualness causes casualties." We cannot be casual about the numbers, for the numbers do not lie.

Here are the areas we focus on at Hubbell Homes:

- Inventory
- Production/Schedule
- Marketing
- Sales
- Financial/Accounting
- Customer Care (Warranty)
- Customer Satisfaction

Each of these areas impacts the others. Without solid marketing, sales will suffer. Without efficient production and schedules, customer satisfaction will suffer. As managers, we must focus on every area. I personally find security in the numbers. They always tell me where to focus my attention. The numbers are my security blanket. I can wrap myself and my business plan around the numbers and feel confident in the future.

Inventory

Inventory tracking for a homebuilder has several main areas: raw land, finished lots, unsold homes under construction, sold homes under construction and finished homes. The key is to focus on the number of lots in front of you as well as land available for further production. Without a dedicated strategy on inventory, it's easy for a builder to be too heavy on land or too light. It's critical to understand where to build, at what price and the absorption of that product.

At Hubbell Homes, we track current sold and unsold inventory by community. We also track sold and unsold inventory by construction phase to better understand any potential bottlenecks for trades.

Finished homes need to be tracked by an *aged inventory* report. A clear, agreed-upon strategy must be in place for any homes not sold within two months and every month thereafter. Birthday homes, which are any homes one year or older, are a major sin. If a home has reached this stage, it comes down to two things--price or people. You are either too proud of your home and refuse to reduce the price or you have the wrong people selling your home. This should be evaluated long before you blow out that candle on the birthday cake.

Production/Schedule

A builder friend from Ohio once told me, "Rachel, you can't close a home if you don't start a home." It may sound obvious, but if you want to hit a certain number of closings, you best make sure you start that many homes at a minimum. Take your number of digs, divide that by your total available months to dig (Iowa winters can be harsh, which prevents digs that make financial sense), which gives you your digs-per-month minimum performance standard. Now, depending where you are in the country, weather can be your friend or foe. For example, on a goal of 200 closings, with nine months to dig, you would strive for a minimum of 22 digs per month. In Iowa, we try to front-load a little and increase the average digs per week, as we usually have some long spells of rain in June or July.

That dig number is then used to determine the production happening *prior* to the dig. Production begins with the initial selection of the home plan and specifications, then moves to drawing, estimating and finally, releasing to the field for digging. If 22 is the monthly goal for digs, six homes need to be selected each week, six drawings per week, and so on. The extra two houses will give needed cushion in case of production shortages in any area on a given week.

Once digging occurs, the construction clock begins to tick. We utilize milestone reports generated from our schedule-management system to better track how long each individual part of the job takes. If there are weather, trade or customer delays, they are notated by using an agreed-upon variance code. This allows for tighter schedule management and transparency throughout the organization.

By focusing on a weekly release number from every area of the start's process, you increase your odds of achieving the illustrious even flow. Even flow is highly desired by trade partners and will help ensure they stay with you as opposed to working for your competition. In today's extreme labor shortage, focusing on creating reliability in work for your trades is a true difference-maker.

Marketing

Marketing is separate from sales because I believe one leads to the other. They are not interchangeable, but they do and must coexist. Many builders try to lump them into the same category, but I don't believe in that method. Tracking for marketing is all about the leading indicators:

- How many people visit your website?
- How long do they spend on your site? What is the bounce rate?
- How many Internet inquiries are you getting?
- How many people walk into your model home?
- How many people share your posts on Facebook? (Notice I didn't say how many people LIKE your posts. Sharing a post will increase your reach exponentially.)
- How many views did your YouTube video receive?
- What is the opening rate of your weekly home e-newsletter?

Over time, you will be able to see trends based on these numbers. For example, if you see a spike in Web traffic, how long does it take for that to translate into an uptick in sales? This is where sales can help marketing by foreseeing and alerting marketing to the trends they see in homeowners/buyers.

Marketing is a process which takes strategy in many forms, from research to visuals, all in the hope that your business will connect with your customer.

Sales

The capture rate of prospects by your sales team is essential. To track this, take the number of written contracts and divide by the number of traffic units during one calendar month.

The major report we track is what we call our *Whiteboard Report*. This name is derived from the fact that back in the day, we tracked all these stats on a dry-erase board. The report looks a little like this:

- Neighborhood
- Closing Goal
- Closings Actual
- Pending Sales
- Under Construction Unsold
- Complete Unsold

This allows you to understand where your issues are on a weekly basis and adjust your strategy accordingly.

Financial/Accounting

Every home counts, and more importantly, every dollar counts. Income statements and balance sheets are the most critical numbers to watch. Income statements tell you how efficiently the organization is run, from sticks and bricks to overhead. The industry-wide standard for minimum performance is a 5% net.

The balance sheet provides critical information to your lenders, such as assets that can be converted to cash within one year and current liabilities. Remember, no real estate company has gone broke from a lack of assets, but rather from a lack of cash.

I do not expect every associate in our organization to know all the financials, but I do expect the following to be known by all for each home:

Gross Margin Prior to Release of a Home

Our standard is never to release a home below a 20% gross margin without prior approval, with 23–25% being the goal. The best production builders reach 28% or more. In order to release a home at a decent margin, it is essential that you know your marketplace. What are your comps? Have you walked the competition to ensure you are comparing apples to apples, so to speak? If you have the right features in the home but can't hit a sales price the market will handle, it isn't worth releasing the home. Never forget, homebuyers don't care what it cost you to build the home, no matter how proud you are of the home.

Gross margin is calculated as follows:

Gross Margin = sales price – total hard cost (includes land but excludes interest and tax)/sales price X 100.

For example, a ranch is listed for $350,000. Hard costs including land total $265,000. ($350,000–$265,000)/$350,000 X 100 = 24.2%.

With the correct numbers upfront, it's easier for the organization to have a shot at a decent net price. Once a home is out the door, cost controls need to be in place to monitor variances and field waste.

Customer Care

Customer care is all about how fast you can complete your open work orders. Any lingering unresolved issues can greatly impact a customer's willingness to refer your business to a friend or family member or to become a repeat-buyer. It's important to track which trades have outstanding work orders and the average days of those open items. This will allow you to address problem trades on a weekly basis. As part of our transparency initiative, we send this report to all trades. It is amazing how many trades don't want to see their company name with large numbers of open work orders or excessive days to complete.

Customer Satisfaction

We utilize a third party to handle customer satisfaction scores. There are many great companies available to choose from, and all track essentially the same items:

- Willingness to refer

- Move-in score
- Mid-year score
- Year-end score

A quality third-party survey company will share with you the national averages and benchmark you against other builders. In addition, surveys can tell you if you have the wrong products in your home, what a customer loved most about the home, how well your sales team did, as well as the mortgage lender, your superintendent, and finally, your customer care team after the sale. Sharing these survey scores throughout your entire team will increase transparency and accountability.

I truly believe that if you wrap yourself in your numbers you will be able to focus your attention where it is needed most. You will gain greater understanding of the business throughout the organization. Use the numbers to reward your teams or encourage non-performers to step it up. Remember, the greatest threat to your business is what happens in your business each and every day. You must know your numbers in order to take it to the next level. One thing is for sure, the numbers never lie!

Take a moment...

- You must know your numbers in order to take your business to the next level.
- The greatest threat to your business is what happens each and every day.
- Every home counts, and more importantly, every dollar counts.

THIS PAGE IS INTENTIONALLY BLANK

Michelle Smallwood took a circuitous route to find her "home" in home building and has been the Vice President of Sales & Marketing at Holiday Builders for the past 11 years. Michelle graduated from Valparaiso University with a BA and went to work for Dun & Bradstreet, where she got her first taste of home building and her interest never waned. From there her extensive management experience and skills earned her a Sales and Service VP role in Florida and then to Operations and Sales Consulting in Scotland, Switzerland, Dominican Republic, El Salvador, Spain, Peru, England, Ireland, all over the US and points beyond. The consulting helped Michelle earn a spot on the Holiday Builders staff and she has never looked back. Michelle has served as the local HBA Sales & Marketing Council chair and also served as a Board Member and Secretary for the Brevard Home Builders & Contractors Assn.

Kathie McDaniel is employed by Holiday Builders as the Corporate Sales and Training Director. Kathie has a passion for sales and training and promotes the NAHB educational courses and designations to everyone she meets in and outside of the industry. She has worked in several major Florida markets for 20 years and was recently recognized as the Woman of Distinction by FHBA. Kathie earned her BA at the University of Toledo and immediately entered the building and real estate industry. She is a dedicated sales and marketing professional who has been involved with the National Association of Home Builders her entire career and holds several designations as well as being a certified instructor for the NAHB.

VP of Sales + Sales Managers = Building a Successful Team

Homebuilders' sales goals are defined by numbers but achieved through relationships. The Vice President of Sales and Marketing and the sales managers are the key players in executing the processes which make the difference between meeting goals and knocking them out of the park. It all begins with these key players setting expectations, establishing clear lines of communication and extending that relationship along the corporate chain.

Too often, a sales manager is hired and given a sales goal with little exposure to the company culture and is provided with limited tools for success. It's kind of like being given a car with directions how to get across town but not enough gas to get there. The sales manager is charged with coaching and developing a sales team, which takes a lot of drive and a lot of fuel. Getting the best mileage from sales managers begins with the VP at the time of recruitment.

HIRING

The VP of Sales knows the key to being a good and effective sales manager starts at the hiring process (not only for the sales manager but also for the team members). The company's culture sets the tone for the sales manager and the type of team needed to assemble. Is there a sales manager candidate within the current sales team or should one be hired from outside the team? Once the company identifies the culture and fit needed for a sales manager, the search begins for the best candidate.

The sales manager's role is critical to the success of the company. They will define the most effective coaching strategy to use to create a successful team. They are responsible for meeting sales goals, fostering the company culture, exceeding customer service goals, maintaining a successful sales team and retaining the team for future growth. Again, the type of manager largely depends on the company's message and culture. In large national companies the manager's role will be quite different than in small local builders managing a handful of salespeople. The type of product the company offers will also play a role in the type of manager needed, because they will need to believe in the product and message in order to effectively lead their sales team.

An experienced VP of Sales and Marketing will hire a sales manager who has the right balance of coaching, mentoring and sales experience and who fits well in the company culture. The VP of Sales is the lead facilitator in familiarizing the sales manager with the nuances of the executive team, the strengths and weaknesses of the organization and the culture that defines the company. The need for mutual respect cannot be underestimated. The VP has the influence with the executive team to ensure marketing and training programs are funded and executed. The sales manager needs the ear of the VP to celebrate and reward sales team achievements and communicate and overcome stumbling blocks in the field. A successful VP of Sales has a good intellect for business and they give the sales manager and their team enthusiasm and attention.

It is important to recruit and hire sales managers who have not only been involved in new home sales--they've been *successful* in selling. It isn't enough to be a good manager--a lack of boots-on-the-ground sales experience will quickly backfire. The sales manager must have credibility to lead and mentor a team. An inexperienced sales manager isn't relatable and ultimately will be exposed by not having the knowledge needed to speak the industry language. This leads to negativity in the ranks and a sales team left to their own devices.

LEADING BY EXAMPLE

The sales manager must lead by example so the message they send to the sales team will be respected and followed by the team. They must require accountability for the team, but also for themselves. If the sales manager asks them to perform a certain task, the sales manager must also master the task. Sales managers lose credibility when the sales team coaches the manager. We ask the sales team to work long hours, to work most or all weekends and to push for excellence in contract preparation and communication. The sales manager needs to lead the charge by being available during the hours the team is working. The sales manager should be present at the sales center on a weekend to show the team they are also in the thick of things and ready to do what it takes to help the team be successful. When the sales manager falls short, they should send an apology or publically admit when they were wrong. Sales managers, don't be above making mistakes--the team will respect you for it. It also sets the tone for them to do the same when and if they fall short.

Industry experts agree that an effective sales manager needs to be in the field and in front of the sales team 90% of the time. Sadly, few companies practice this formula. Sales managers end up in countless meetings and pushing paper instead of spending their time teaching and motivating. Holiday Builders puts the onus of managerial meetings on the VP of Sales and Marketing, leaving the sales manager free to spend one-on-one time with sales team members.

The sales manager is trained to understand the processes and reports used by the executive team. Again, a clear and communicative relationship between the VP and the sales manager ensures the executive team is well-informed and able to gauge projections and the sales team is well-positioned to achieve sales goals. This is a macro-to-micro management style.

When working in the field, the sales manager should plan and schedule visits with sales team members in advance so time away from model centers is kept to a minimum. The meetings should include compliments, encouragement and rewards for effort and current results and should end by addressing any areas in need of improvement and a recommendation of how to improve skills and become more successful. Sales managers need to employ the same method of conducting business with team members as the

VP does with the sales manager. Keeping coaching sessions short and focused and handling other communication via email and phone calls allows the sales team to focus on customer service and sales. Less time in meetings allows the sales team to work their pipeline, put coaching plans to increase sales into practice and achieve the desired results.

Use empathy! At their core, sales managers are people managers. Having the ability to empathize with the sales team will show them actual caring and that they are more than simply a revenue stream. Each team member is different. Demonstrating the ability to understand current life situations, motivations and goals help a manager achieve buy-in and trust, which in turn easily drives productivity. And remember, when hiring a sales team, one size does not fit all! Diversity and variety in a sales team will attract more buyers. This means the manager needs to embrace personality differences and be flexible in his or her approach to coaching. The sales manager must earn the trust of the team, so the ability to coach to each person's different personality and skill level is imperative.

Striving for excellence is a widely-used phrase. It can be achieved by having a strategic plan and taking structured action to help others be successful. Leading from the top down at all points in the company offers a great opportunity to mentor and lead by example. The VP is always the final decision-maker and leader of collaborative conversations with the team, listening to every side of every circumstance and making decisions beneficial to the entire organization. The experienced sales manager trains, mentors and rewards the sales team, ensuring success time after time. Sales team members witness the success of their peers and stay inspired to achieve goals. Expectations, processes and clear communication, established at the onset from VP to sales manager to the sales team members, are the most effective tools for success.

SALES ENVIRONMENT

A leading sales manager will create a positive sales environment. Salespeople tend to be transparent and wear their emotions openly. When they have a personal struggle, it's apparent to others and can cause interference in sales. A good sales manager will identify personal issues and help their team members through those times by creating a positive environment. Always ask each team member how their day is going and what's going on in their personal lives. Know them personally, and address issues that may take away their focus. Let them know they are important and they will want to deliver top performance. Reward the little things with praise and reward the top performers on a regular basis. Monthly, quarterly and annual awards are a good way to recognize the team. Team members will strive to achieve the coveted role of top-selling agent to be recognized with the award. Recognition by the sales manager will funnel through to the sales team and they will start to recognize each other for achievements.

COACHING

Coaching the team is different than managing and a good sales manager will do both. Managing requires constant review of the company's policies and procedures. Is the team meeting the guidelines for the practices set by the company in maintaining the model and sales center? Are they at work on time, showing up prepared to get to work? Is their paperwork in order with little or no errors? Every company has an employee handbook or policies in place and it's the sales manager's role to manage and enforce them.

Coaching is exactly what the title says--be a coach to the team. Motivate them, inspire them, push them to exceed and hold them accountable for failures or when they aren't giving 100%. Conduct practice sessions by role playing and regular training in order to seek improvement. Practice often, train often and create a culture of excellence.

When coaching, look for specific talents in each individual. Identify their differences and in which areas each person excels, and then help them build on those skills. A good sales manager knows their team intimately and will identify the salespeople who want more than a sales career. However, all good salespeople will not make good sales managers. If a salesperson is identified by a manager as having other career goals, the manager can groom them to fit within the company in that role. Being a mentor to a team member will create a bond that is not easily broken. Develop the team to either be a successful sales team or be great at doing something else within the company. Don't let the team consider moving to another company to meet their personal goals.

An effective sales manager should be a mentor who challenges and inspires growth in all of their team members. He or she should be someone who is respected and has an outstanding and accomplished history. On top of amazing interpersonal skills, they must also have the ability to be candid and direct, as salespeople tend to respect those who explain their thought processes versus directing without explanation. Are you a manager who constantly compliments the team? The sales team will look forward to a good sales manager's visits.

A good manager will exhibit consistent behavior in all situations, yet the tone is set by the circumstance. When sales are short, the manager will be a driving force at the end of the month and the team will come to expect it. The message will be clear and the team will react. The same manager will reward and respond to the team openly and excitingly when sales soar past their goals in a given period and the team will continue to strive to beat sales. When coaching or training is needed or the company has a business communication, the manager will take the lead with a professional and serious demeanor. Consistency in behavior will build consistency in sales.

The best managers in the world never forget where they came from. Many of the least likable managers are ones who forgot how hard their first years in sales were. The best leaders understand the struggles and *stay in the trenches*. If a sales manager is ready to keep getting their hands dirty and win and lose with their team, they'll be great.

Think about it--if a sales manager contradicts these points and values, what type of sales manager will they be? A sales manager who stays at the office behind the desk and computer screen will not be engaged with the team. The team will be left to their own devices, creating an environment of chaos. They will have nothing to build on, nobody to build team excitement or push them, nobody to guide and shape them, nobody to motivate them or drive them and not a single sales person will perform, let alone stay long in this environment. Salespeople need direction and like to be pushed beyond their expectations. Hire the manager who will drive sales, manage the process and coach for excellence.

Take a Moment...

1. Lead by example--be passionate, motivating and have a high sense of integrity.
2. Build the team by coaching and motivating them. Give constant feedback, praise and rewards, but discipline when appropriate.
3. Create a culture of consistency.
4. Be a mentor. Identify each team member's niche and help them build on it!

Erica Lockwood joined the Joseph Chris Partners team in September 2000 and has since excelled within the company and the industry where she is well known for being a leading executive search professional. In Erica's current role as Equity/Executive Partner, she helps support company initiatives, talent development and plays an active role in business development.

What makes Erica unparalleled as an executive search professional is her capacity to identify exceptional talent. Her perseverance and ability to understand each individual client's needs have allowed her to complete some extremely tough searches. Becoming a true strategic partner with her clients has created countless long-term relationships with companies who utilize her expertise year after year.

When she isn't focused on filling her client's searches, you will most likely find Erica enjoying spending time with her friends and family at her lake home, kayaking or driving her Jeep Wrangler.

Winning the Edge and Building Your Team Roster

Football. It's a big deal in my house. I mean a *really* big deal. Football season is not just about faithfully attending and watching the regular season games and, if luck is on our side, cheering for our favorite teams in the conference playoffs or beyond. We also closely follow the NFL Combine, NFL Draft, and team training camps the way some people binge-watch the latest series on Netflix. There is one incredibly clear observation throughout the events leading up to the first kickoff of football season--the level of pure talent and determination found in the athletes is nothing less than incredible.

As a real-estate industry *talent scout*, I readily recognize the need for the endless pursuit to identify the next team of recruits and future leaders. The Combine and Draft activities have many similarities to building teams in business. Let me grab my virtual clipboard and share some thoughts from my playbook.

I had the opportunity to attend a day at the NFL Combine earlier this year. The atmosphere was unique and nothing like the regular sights and sounds I have grown accustomed to under the Lucas Oil Stadium roof. It was honestly more like a mix  between a golf match and a visit to the library. Imagine all 32 NFL team representatives present with an overall vibe of *this is* **SERIOUS** *business*. No talking, no movement during drills. *Serious business*.

The NFL Combine not only highlights each athlete's college stats. The draft hopefuls perform additional testing and skills evaluations during the almost week-long job interview-of-all-interviews. Although the screening process looks a bit different from that in the business world, there are some useful lessons to take from the Combine experience.

1. **It's Not all about Stats.** During the Combine, there are many on-field drills. However, there are also interviews and written tests. Teams are evaluating the athletes and looking into individual thought processes. Just because a player has an amazing resume of college statistics does not necessarily mean a perfect fit for a team, or the league for that matter--can you say Johnny Manziel? Teams are typically looking for well-rounded *and* grounded athletes, not an individual who may have above-average game stats but presents some red flags which could be detrimental to the team functionality.

How often have you looked at a resume and made a quick evaluation as to whether the person would be a good fit? It is a well-known fact that the average recruiter or hiring manager reviews a resume in six seconds or less. Are you passing on potential candidates because their resumes don't look perfect at first blush? Or are you looking at potential new hires solely based on their results and not fully delving into their fit within your overall culture and current team? Those little red flags we have all been guilty of ignoring can potentially cause a negative affect within the team. As you screen and hire talent at any level, you must consider attitude and aptitude, not educational background or current company or title alone. Along with this, there should be a formal testing component to any hiring process. There are many options available in the marketplace, but one thing is certain--hiring managers will attest to the validity of assessments and the short and long-term differences formed by those hiring decisions. The cost of making a bad hiring decision has more connected to it than a monetary value, and the lessons associated with those hires should be assessed and reassessed often. After all, the definition of insanity is doing the same thing repeatedly and expecting a different outcome. Being caught in a fourth-down situation regularly is not a position of strength!

2. **Not all Talent Comes from the Best-Known Schools.** I always find it interesting to learn about the incoming NFL draft hopefuls' backgrounds. While most do come from the more well-known universities, there are many who have made a splash and created positive attention related to their raw talent and potential. I believe it is human nature to look favorably upon talent from a bigger school or a larger company background. Does this always make an incredible fit within an organization or team? Tony Romo, for instance, a Dallas Cowboy quarterback superstar, was drafted from Eastern Illinois University. Likewise, my very own Indianapolis Colts Kicker, Adam Vinatieri, came from South Dakota State. Both NFL stars have made an incredible impact within the league and did so overcoming initial judgement based on the credibility of their collegiate background.

How often are you overlooking talent from smaller companies or educational backgrounds differing from your expectations? Sometimes we may need to set aside the official job description and look at the whole picture to see the possibilities. While you can't argue with the facts and data that demonstrate excellent talent regularly emerges from the top construction-management-focused universities, there are endless exceptions to that rule. A similar scenario can occur when assumptions are made that the best and brightest candidates can only be found within the largest publicly-traded builders and in the major metro markets where they are conducting business. I can think of many examples of shining stars I identified throughout my career who were working within a smaller company and/or were located within a secondary or tertiary market. Each was happily working in their current role, unaware of the amazing opportunity I was about to present. My own personal version of a Quarterback Sneak play!

3. **Not all Talent Appears to be Perfect.** The 2018 NFL Combine proved to be quite interesting. Several new records were set by various athletes, but this was nothing in comparison to a young man's story about overcoming adversity. Shaquem Griffin, former UCF Linebacker, arrived at the 2018 NFL Combine in the same manner as his athlete peers, but he did so without his left hand. Though he'd had his left hand amputated at four years old, Shaquem never let his imperfection stop him from being the best he could be. Amazingly, he ran the fastest 40-yard dash by a linebacker *ever* in NFL Combine history. I was thrilled to be present to witness such an amazing feat. In addition, he had 20 reps on the 225-pound bench press during the Combine using a prosthetic arm. He is now playing alongside his twin brother, Shaquill, for the Seattle Seahawks. Talk about an inspiring example of sheer willpower and determination!

As I consider the lack of talent currently available within our industry, I cannot help but think about my daily conversations related to the detrimental effects this situation is creating in our universe. Where will the new talent come from and how will the industry respond should significant change not occur? As a linebacker without a left hand was offered the chance to realize his life-long dream to become a professional football player, perhaps part of our hiring process should include potential candidates who may not present with all the right tools or required qualifications.

What if a candidate has the passion and desire to be the best version of themselves and go above and beyond? You will not be able to assess that based on reviewing a resume for six seconds alone. You may need to consider those who present with more than just the usual resume submission. As an example, I have an amazing long-time client who gives preference to candidates who submit a well-written cover letter/introduction along with a resume when responding to a job posting. This stellar builder has successfully hired and retained some of the industry's best talent and has transformed their culture into one with a highly-regarded reputation within their local market. The intentionality of knowing what a unique candidate looks like is key to having the ability to pursue those individuals. Likewise, let's not forget the Unrestricted Free Agents in the workforce. I believe there are tried and true gems out there who only need an opportunity to shine within a company that recognizes individual contributions and awards excellence. Much of this talent pool may be overlooked, which is unfortunate given the lack of current talent options and the expertise and skills this group of professionals can bring to the table.

Other options for outside-of-the-box candidate sourcing include schoolteachers who often make some of the greatest salespeople. These professionals are detail-oriented and have the exposure to helping individuals through a process of learning and understanding. Likewise, retail candidates working within high-demand selling environments with little-or-no additional compensation are also great potential candidates. The options are certainly out there, and we as industry professionals must seek out those with potential and consider how we can make a smooth transition occur. We ought to be sure everything in our power has been done to create a roadmap for success.

I strongly believe there is a common goal within all company leadership teams to build a successful roster of talent who possess the ability not only to meet but to smash both individual and company goals. An important component in creating this dream team is to be mindful of aligning talent within skillsets and company cultures. From time to time, you can find examples of NFL players who were not the best choice for a team based on the culture or coaching style. That same player may excel exceptionally well under other leadership regimes. It is truly all a part of being mindful of the role you are wanting to fill and the talent which you believe will be most effective in that role based on a variety of factors and not just a resume or gut feeling.

Building a team, whether in football or in our amazing industry, takes tenacity, intentional networking and communication and a desire to never take shortcuts when it comes to acquiring talent. When you have secured the right people in the right positions, success is inevitable!

"My number one priority, and it always has been this, is keeping our team together and making sure we have the right guys in the right positions to make a run at this for a long time."
– Drew Brees

Are You Guilty of *Out-Kicking Your Coverage?*

This football terminology applies to either a kicker or a punter. When a kicker is in a situation where he must kick the ball downfield and ultimately his teammates are not there to make a tackle and cover the kick, they lose their advantage. At least one player ultimately did not follow the plan, leaving everyone else in the dust and ending up giving the advantage to the opposing team. In the business world, this scenario may apply to the hasty hiring process or lack of a definitive assessment process which creates confusion or mayhem. This kind of situation may create erosion of teamwork and often causes a loss of momentum.

I believe this situation can be avoided by having a defined hiring process and a committed team of players who are in tune with the company objectives related to talent acquisition. Do you have a defined hiring team who can make critical decisions related to new hires? The initial hiring process is a critical component of our business and it's crucial to have the right people in charge of this task. Just as important as the hiring process are your onboarding tasks. Nothing says, "Welcome to the team, we sure weren't ready for you this morning," than an ill-devised onboarding process.

Is Your Quarterback (Hiring Manager) Able and Ready to Call an Audible?

Once a quarterback gets the game plan from their coach, their job is to bring it to the rest of the team. There are times when the game doesn't go according to plan and the quarterback must adjust on the fly. The hiring manager also has the responsibility for adjusting strategy and rallying the team related to the new direction. Having a defined set of expectations and support for the hiring manager and their overall decisions can make or break the hiring process. In today's fast-paced hiring environment, you must CRUSH the two-minute drill. One minute it may look like your candidate is ready and totally on board to join the team. And then the counter-offer happens. This is when time kills a deal and your hiring manager needs to know they can move quickly and not lose the game. It is imperative the hiring manager is confident in their direction and authority to do so.

Making Halftime Adjustments is Completely Acceptable.

Bill Belichick is famously known for his halftime adjustments. He is also known for saying, "A plan is great until you actually get into battle, and then it doesn't mean anything." Making adjustments for the sake of making adjustments isn't practical. When you must make adjustments, be sure they're in line with the guiding principles which have been set in place and communicated to the team. In today's market, the need to be nimble and creative is not an option. Does your hiring team have a clear direction and the authority to make halftime adjustments if the need arises? Just as the second half of a game is critical, the final pieces of the hiring process are just as significant. The power of the hiring team to execute without delay can make or break the ability to bring top talent to your team.

While we all know there is no "I" in the word team, the I-formation play is key to having a dominant offensive run. Each of the players knows their job and executes the play. This is the essence of teamwork that leads to a win!

Nationally-acclaimed Design Studio Expert, **Jane Meagher**, has worked with hundreds of builders in more than 42 states and Canada to increase option sales and improve homebuyer experiences. Jane's company, Success Strategies, has created approximately 160 unique design studio environments and won 24 National Awards for "Best Design Center" from NAHB. Jane has been a highly rated, featured speaker at NAHB's International Builders Show for over 20 years. She has spoken at virtually every major homebuilding industry conference. Jane's unparalleled credentials and years of wide-ranging expertise make her uniquely positioned to convey an in-depth mastery of the design studio world.

Jane is a homebuilding industry Strategist, applying consumer purchase psychology, retail theory, global consumer insights, product and pricing strategies, sales and influence strategies, and decision-making theory to homebuilder design studio operations for the purposes of providing world-class customer experiences and increasing revenue and profit.

Nationally Recognized Speaker and Trainer. Jane is a popular and dynamic speaker and has been a featured or keynote speaker at almost 100 industry conferences and events.

Published/Featured Author. In addition to previously writing a popular blog entitled "Think like a Consumer/Act like a Retailer"® for Builder Magazine/Hanley Wood, Jane has been published and/or quoted in many leading publications.

Profit by Design

How do we support our customer in creating a uniquely personalized home that satisfies their lifestyle needs and design preferences without losing control of the homebuying process?

Today's homebuyer walks into your sales center with an iced-venti, sugar-free mocha soy latte with extra whipped cream in one hand and in her other hand, a cell phone which has been personalized 100 different ways--from the font size to the screen brightness to the order of the icons--and she doesn't want to be told that on the most expensive and emotional purchase of her lifetime, someone else made all the decisions that she now must "live with"... figuratively and literally.

Most builders think like construction companies who are focused on building high-quality homes. And of course that is critical. But what if builders thought like retailers of the most expensive item someone may ever buy--a well-constructed new home? That's a paradigm shift that will change perspective, decisions and results.

When we look at how deeply embedded personalization is for today's consumers in virtually all product and service categories and the heightened customer focus of leading brands, coupled with the financial opportunity for homebuilders to capture more high-margin dollars on every precious home sale, it's no wonder that builders are obsessively focusing today on how buyers personalize their homes.

Whether you're exploring improvements to the physical environment of your design studio, striving toward replicable operational best practices, maximizing the sales and design teams' performance, or optimizing the products and pricing of your optional products, there are four overarching goals to keep in mind.

How do you:

- Deliver a world-class customer experience? (Thrill and delight your buyers with an unparalleled buying experience.)
- Maximize per-home revenue? (Don't leave money on the table. Capture the most high-profit revenue dollars on every single home you sell.)
- Streamline internal operations? (Create replicable, fair, enforceable policies and procedures that reflect industry best practices and provide a foundation for success.)
- Leverage your design studio and personalization experience as a compelling reason to buy from you? (Attract prospective buyers aligned with your brand and personalization promise and more quickly and easily convert prospects to buyers.)

To discover how you can reach these goals, you'll need to consider the 5 Ps of Personalization:

- Product and Pricing: (the "WHAT") Sell the right products, the right amount of products, at the right price
- Policies and Procedures: (the "HOW") The structure and framework for the personalization experience
- Place: (the "WHERE") The environment in which the personalization experience unfolds
- People: (the "WHO") The front-line design (and sales teams who deliver the personalization experience
- Promotion: (the "WHY") How you use the personalization experience to uphold your brand promise and attract the right buyers to your company

Product and Pricing

It all starts with this question: What are you selling in your design-studio store?

If you don't get that answer right, then none of your other endeavors are going to reach their maximum potential and you will jeopardize your overarching goals. There's a fallacy that the way to delight your customers is to offer them everything and never say NO. Research, both in and out of our industry, has conclusively proved that to be false. The path of least resistance is to offer everything your supplier drops off and avoid the hard work of SKU rationalization. The smart builder realizes that quantity of choice affects decision-making in multiple ways: decision-making speed, decision confidence, customer spend and ultimate satisfaction. Today's leading builders evaluate sales and customer data, design trends, profit potential, product applicability and other factors to make strategic decisions about which and how many products to offer. They update continually to stay not just on top of the trends, but where applicable, out in front of them.

Product Assortment is a retailing term for the breadth and depth of your Included and Optional features. Your Product Assortment goal is to offer the right products, the right amount of products, pre-priced and pre-vetted, and slotted into levels wherever possible, so it's easy for your customer to say YES. Here are some of the many factors to consider: sales history (industry-wide, geographically, and with your own past customer history), trends (your customers expect you to be a design leader), applicability, warranty, revenue and profit potential and coordination with both your floorplans and with other products you offer.

When it comes to pricing, don't be so pragmatic. Cost plus a certain percentage is a factor to consider, not an end point. Instead, price to consumer demand and apply psychological pricing strategies. The key is in not thinking like a construction company. Consider how your customer is going to determine value (a perception which you can significantly influence) and what that value will be. You don't have to be "cheaper" than retail...you need to offer a Better Overall Value. Act like a world-class retailer when making those all-important pricing decisions.

Policies and Procedures

Now that you know what you want to sell in your store, how are you going to sell it?

Policies are the rules of engagement for your customer and your company to work together harmoniously and successfully. A few examples are:

- What **deposit** is required for option sales, and when is it due?
- What is your **change order** (we call it "Late Change Request") policy around buyers asking to change the items they already "signed off" on? (We call this "Authorizing and Finalizing".)
- What is your **custom request** (we call it "Special Request") policy? What happens when your buyer wants an item outside of your predefined menu of choice, i.e., outside your Product Assortment Scope?
- How many hours of preview, design appointment and open-house time are available or required?
- How does information flow between your design studio and other departments?
- How are expectations set for your customers? Are they repeated more than once through various methods? Are they properly communicated? Enforced? Are your **policies** fair and appropriate?
- Do you have the appropriate control required to run an efficient building company or are your customers running the show?
- Are your policies buyer-friendly enough to allow your customers to have a highly-satisfactory experience or do your buyers feel forced into unreasonable builder-focused rules and regulations?
- Are your policies consistent with your brand image and competitive position in the marketplace?
- Are your policies designed to support your business goals TODAY? (Hint: If you haven't reevaluated this in years,

they are likely NOT aligned with today's homebuilding climate, your current staffing or today's homebuying customer.)

Procedures are the actions which execute your policies and operational standards. This includes exactly how your design studio operates and how both the customers and the design studio team members interact with all other departments in your company.

- How do you set **expectations** around your policies and your operational standards so your buyers' experiences meet or exceed their expectations? (That's the definition of customer satisfaction.)
- What specific action steps, and in what order, are needed to carry out those procedures?
- Does the sales team understand it is their responsibility to set up the customer for a successful design studio experience? Do they make sure the customer TRULY understands the included features and knows what to expect, plus when and how the upcoming personalization experience will unfold? To prohibit the customer suffering from the sales and design team operating as silos, the sales team must also deliver specific customer data and insights to the design team...for every single buyer, every single time.
- Who needs to be involved in every action, step and procedure? The design studio is not an island unto itself, isolated from the rest of the company customers visit on their way to their final destination. If you think of the design studio as an island, then picture it as being surrounded by the land masses of your other departments (sales, marketing, construction, estimating, purchasing, architecture, accounting, closing, customer care and management) with boats travelling constantly through the Island of the Design Studio, carrying team members and customers to and from every direction. All departments

must function cohesively as one common group bonded together through continual customer focus. Regarding operational best practices for how builders handle their options program and buyer personalization experience, builders are often surprised to find that only half of the solution is about what occurs inside the design studio during buyer visits and appointments. The other half is what occurs throughout the rest of your building company before, during and after the buyer's direct interaction with the design studio.

Tools are the paper or digital documents, physical elements, etc., which are required to effectively carry out these action steps. Do you have the proper drawings, comprehensive enhanced option descriptions, product samples and other tools your customers need to be successful at complying with your stated policies and deadlines?

Do the many legal and marketing documents used throughout presentation and selection of optional products protect both the business and the customer from potentially disastrous mistakes and conflicting interpretations?

Documented design studio policies and procedures ensure consistent, replicable best practices. They protect you from the "my design consultant quit and I wish I knew more about how she actually did things in there" syndrome. Your business will run smoothly and efficiently when your entire team (sales, marketing, design, estimating, purchasing, construction, customer care/warranty, and upper management) has a concrete understanding of what is supposed to happen, why, and how it is supposed to unfold. Include your customers in that understanding, and you'll have a recipe for top-notch customer satisfaction. Clarity around policies and procedures will reduce or eliminate frustrated or dissatisfied customers AND team member inefficiency.

Place

Perception is Reality. We must present our strategically derived

Product Assortment to our customers in a way which increases perceived value rather than depresses it. Your customers' determination of value is something you CAN significantly impact. If you don't believe that the quality of your physical presentation can drive or prohibit product sales, then I invite you to explore the roles of context, perception, sequencing and connection in evaluating value.

Every day your customers experience world-class retailing environments at their local malls, where they are purposefully influenced to interact with products in ways that produce an optimized result and a "yes" purchase decision. In these high-quality retail environments, customers are immersed in a heightened ambiance designed to focus their attention and emotions on the store's products. Customers are put in the mood to buy very specific types of products through strong emotional connections and proof-of-product benefits and value.

Customers often unknowingly wander along a pathway purposefully designed to unfold a strategically-determined sequence of products that will maximize their total spend.

Site-lines and pathways based on behavioral science principles and retailing best practices create a sequential buying pathway designed to optimize revenue-per-customer.

Products are packaged and displayed in fixtures that not only align with the store's brand, but also put the focus on the product, encouraging the buyer to physically connect with the products in ergonomically optimal ways. Ultimately, the store facilitates a connection that leads to an almost impossible-to-resist purchase decision. Customers are provided with everything they need to say "yes" by removing potential psychological roadblocks to a purchase. Retailers know how to overcome roadblocks such as lack of clarity, customer overwhelm, and fear of overpaying.

You must act like a retailer, manufacture desire and create a compelling ambiance. Your customer doesn't think, "Oh, wow, this place just has piles of products and a mishmash of racks thrown up against the walls, but that's okay because this is a homebuilder's store." They actually think, "Wow, considering I'll spend more money here than at any store I've visited, this is pretty low quality. The sales center was so cool but now that I've bought from them, it sure doesn't look like the builder really thought much about my experience. It kind of feels like they just want me to pick some stuff and be done. I was excited at first, but now I feel frustrated and uninspired. I didn't expect this subpar situation because otherwise they seemed to be pretty on top of things."

Some builders settle for a haphazard "selections area" with a mishmash of vendor-provided displays of every shape, size and color that have zero connection to the builder's brand--and which ultimately creates visual overload, loss of focus, decreased perceived value and tons of wasted time and energy for all involved. Smart homebuilders realize they need to create a compelling environment, which proudly presents their high-quality products to today's savvy shoppers.

Even if a room in a model home is the best you can do for your "design center" you can still employ the principles described herein to the best of your ability and make it as great as you can.

However, a true "design studio" requires more than a 10x10 room to become a retail environment filled with the tools that influence both sides of a customer's decision-making brain. To influence the "left-directed brain", you'll need properly-located, high-quality, ergonomically-correct displays which allow the buyer to easily digest and comprehend the scope of choice, and to compare and contrast products in a way which leads to quick, easy and confident decisions. A "design studio" must also provide right-brain-directed tools such as vignettes, which are simulated real-life environments providing contextual cues for how the products will fit together in the buyer's home, i.e., how they look when installed with other products. These immersive vignette elements manufacture desire and create emotion strong enough to propel the sale forward.

It's no wonder when our builder clients open design studios or improve their policies and procedures, they realize how much high-margin revenue was being left on the table. After implementing improvements, builders are often shocked to discover that their buyers are investing more dollars into their brand new homes than was ever thought possible, and their customer satisfaction has gone up simultaneously, now that they are more connected to their own unique homes.

It's not enough to have a high-quality environment and best-in-class procedures. Ultimately it comes down to the quality of the interaction between your design consultant and your buyers.

People

Once you have operational standards, they won't do much good if they are not communicated to your customers in a buyer-friendly way, in concrete, digestible terms, all the time. All the right products in a beautiful state-of-the-art design studio will mean nothing if they are not presented to our customers in a way which compels them to say YES and be highly-satisfied and excited to do so.

Your design team spends as much as, if not more, time with your customers than your sales team does. They have the power to make or break your design studio success. They need to be able to successfully develop rapport and trust, build desire for your products, communicate the value of your products, overcome objections and answer dozens of questions on hundreds of ever-changing products. Today's uber-educated buyer will quickly turn to other information sources if your team doesn't have the product knowledge and presentation skills required to satisfy buyers' thirst for immediate and accurate information.

Promotion

If you think of your design studio as a place buyers pop into for a few hours between the purchase agreement and the home start, then you are missing the concept of how a true design studio is a critically-important element in your overall business model. Why create a phenomenal environment, aligned with and supporting your brand image, and save it only for buyers who have already purchased from you? Leading builders are front-loading the concept of personalization as a USP (Unique Selling Proposition) by leveraging it as a compelling reason to buy a home in the first place. The archaic, linear pathway of homebuying is long, long gone. Today's consumers experience digital, physical and even virtual shopping in any order they please--often simultaneously--and smart homebuilders are totally on board with that revolutionary concept. Prospective buyers visiting a world-class design studio immediately understand the builder 1) is undeniably focused on creating the ultimate customer experience, 2) is a design leader with the capability to make the customer's dream home become reality and 3) has the resources to deliver what the customer craves...transparency, ease, confidence, expert guidance and even FUN throughout the homebuying and personalization journey. Every day, builders are closing home sales IN the 150+ design studios we've created around the country.

Whether you've got a state-of-the-art design studio environment, a strategically-derived product assortment sure to delight your buyers, a phenomenal customer-focused personalization experience led by expert design consultants--or all of the above--make sure your customers know it up front. Successful builders are attracting more of the type of customer who is better-aligned with their personalization promise and abilities and then delivering on those matched expectations to create evangelical buyers who are raving fans.

To thrive as a builder today, you need to Think Like A Consumer and Act Like A Retailer® to unlock the hidden potential waiting inside your design studio.

THIS PAGE IS INTENTIONALLY BLANK

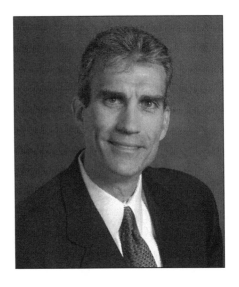

Charlie Scott has more than 30 years of first-hand home building industry's experience as a builder and as President of Woodland, O'Brien & Scott, one of the home building's original customer satisfaction, consulting and referral sales generation firms. Charlie has worked with the Who's Who among U.S. homebuilders and helped guide these builders to operational excellence. As a result, these builders racked up substantial market share growth, higher employee satisfaction and scores of Builder of The Year, America's Best Builder and National Housing Quality Awards.

Charlie is a frequent national and international keynote speaker, National Housing Quality Award Executive Council Member, Contributing Editor for Professional Builder Magazine and author of "Construction Knowledge 101."

Building a Customer-Centric Culture To Maximize Referral Sales

Every homebuilder likes to think their company measures up well when it comes to customer satisfaction. But it doesn't appear to be as easy to evaluate customer satisfaction for new homes as it is for products which naturally generate lots of repeat business. However, industry analysis shows one measure of total customer satisfaction--the percentage of sales originating from customer referrals--can provide both a true estimate of overall customer satisfaction as well as future sales.

The correlation of customer satisfaction and higher sales is documented in multiple studies, most significantly in *Strategy Mapping* by Kenneth A Merchant and Xiaoling Chen, 2009. A well-run homebuilding company can realistically produce a 40+% referral sales rate while simultaneously reducing costs. This is a potent combination for both increasing market share and offering protection during future market downturns.

With 40+% of annual sales at stake, why are so many builders oblivious of their referral sales rate? How can a factor this important be virtually ignored? It may be because homebuilders traditionally have a strong focus on product, or *what* they build (their floor plans) and less focus on their process, or *how* they build (the customer experience).

Homebuilders are extremely adept at designing floor plans to respond to demographic trends which support sales. Floor plans are meticulously scrutinized and detailed to make it easy to build a number of homes at a time, quickly and well in the field. If someone offered homebuilders a floor plan guaranteed to sell 40+% of next year's homes, every homebuilder would jump all over it. Well, there is a plan, but it is *not* a traditional floor plan--it is a homegrown customer experience plan. And as the studies show, this experience plan deserves to receive as much time and effort as an entire new product line.

Building the Customer-Satisfaction Experience

How do we become more customer-centric and design and implement our best-imaginable homebuyer experience? Let's talk about this goal in terms of a three-legged stool.

The First Leg: Recognizing and Meeting Customer Needs

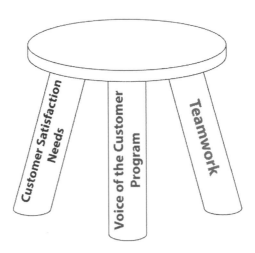

When designing a customer experience plan, you first need to understand the fundamental hierarchy of customer-satisfaction needs. The best way to do that is to review the well-known Abraham Maslow paper, *A Theory of Human Motivation*. What does Maslow's motivation have to do with homebuilding? Everything! We want our customers to be motivated to refer us to their family members and friends. Maslow's paper serves as a proxy to describe the ascending order of needs which must be met in order to produce this referral motivation. We can follow Maslow's hierarchy to build a comparable hierarchy of homebuyer needs. Let's start at the bottom of his pyramid and work our way up.

Abraham Maslow vs. Home Buyer Hierarchy of Needs

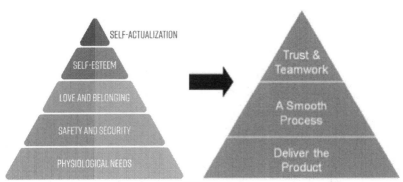

#1 Physiological and Safety Needs

The two lowest levels of Maslow's pyramid, basic needs, equate to the home itself. Here homebuyers are looking for a good home, well-built, with safe products used. The home building corollary is an exquisitely clean and complete home. The home should 100% represent the promise your company's brand pledges: a brand new, move-in ready (inside and outside) home, with all the features, selections and the information necessary for the homeowner to enjoy their new home.

There is nothing else as important as the delivery of a clean and complete home, which is why this is a basic need. This, the biggest customer experience failure, insult and confidence-shaker a builder can commit is 100% in control of the homebuilder, so that has to be priority one. Remember, even the best fix is not as good as getting it right the first time.

#2 Psychological Needs

Maslow describes the psychological needs as primarily regarding relationships. The homebuilding corollary is a good customer experience. This means more than hiring nice people to work for you. It requires a plan to create a consistent and predictable customer experience. Just think what would happen if a homebuilder had no floor plans to reference when building a home. Undoubtedly every home, even starting with the same model, would be built differently. Similarly, leaving customer experience to chance is too high a risk when you consider the cost in lost referrals.

Smart homebuilders produce a consistent customer experience plan to guarantee all staff members know their roles and responsibilities and then work as a team to shepherd the customer through the buying, building and living experience. Really smart builders include a Referral Sales Strategy as part of this plan, as well.

#3 Self-fulfillment Needs

Maslow describes this as *achieving one's potential.* The homebuilding corollary to this is living in a home which was a joy to build with a great experience and ongoing relationships with all the individuals involved. The highest level can be reached by creating an ongoing feeling of trust and appreciation with your homeowners. This is the key to catapulting referral sales into the stratosphere. Unfortunately, too many homebuilders have the perspective that they are done at the time of closing, whereas the customer feels like the relationship should continue. The customer doesn't just expect warranty service, they also want the relationships to survive, if not thrive, after move-in. A customer who feels like the builder doesn't care after closing, or who figuratively loved and then left, is not likely to generate future referral sales.

These customer expectations require a builder's customer experience plan to include post-closing service AND several staff touchpoints to keep that hard-earned great reputation intact and maximize future referral sales.

The Second Leg: Measuring Customer Satisfaction

Having the plan is just one leg of the three-legged stool to higher customer satisfaction and referral sales. The second leg is implementing the plan. This means teaching all the staff members their roles and responsibilities and then monitoring and measuring their individual and team performances. This approach is not uncommon in homebuilding, as it is very similar to creating scopes of work and performance criteria for each trade partner building the home. Likewise, each company team member (Sales, Selections, Construction, Administrative, Closing and Warranty) should have a very clear set of instructions on what they are to teach and deliver to the customer. Once these roles and responsibilities are known by the staff, it is time to measure how well the staff is performing via a Voice-of-the-Customer program.

A well-designed Voice-of-the-Customer (VOC) program is MUCH more than just a customer satisfaction survey. A well-designed VOC gives the homebuilder an objective level of feedback on the performance of individual (and collective) team members and should also allow for customer suggestions for improvement. Generally speaking, the rating questions (i.e. *Please rate home cleanliness on a scale from 1 to 5*) provide the objective/rational customer feedback. On the other hand, experience questions (i.e. *Please share your overall comments, feelings and suggestions)* capture the subjective/emotional concerns of the customers. And smart builders include an important follow-up question after, *Are you willing to refer your family and friends?* They ask, *How many family and friends have you referred?* and assure the onsite salespeople regularly receive and maintain great relationships with their highest-referring homeowners.

Studies show that tasking a third party to perform the VOC is the better way to go. Internal surveys are significantly less accurate. Almost half of all customers wish to remain anonymous, so a direct survey forces at least half of the respondents to falsify their feedback. Homeowners generally don't want to risk damaging a relationship, especially when their upcoming warranty service may be at stake. Thus, they invoke the safe *everything was fine* response. With these false-positive conditioned responses, homebuilders with internally-administered surveys are almost always under the impression they are performing well and are unaware of their less than customer-centric processes and people.

A well-designed VOC survey can be anywhere from 30 to 80 questions in length, and if presented properly, can achieve response rates of 60-70%, which is more than sufficient for statistical accuracy. Experience shows that customers will invest up to two hours of survey/feedback time, IF they believe their homebuilder is genuine in their desire for honest feedback. An internally-administered survey is often interpreted as a sign the request is not really genuine. For example, think how we all feel when a company, say an auto dealership asks, "Is there any reason you can't give me a 5 on my customer service today? My bonus depends on all 5's." We universally hate this approach and we begin to feel the feedback is for a selfish reason and not genuinely seeking honesty, right?

Timing is also important when attempting to capture meaningful customer feedback. The best time for customer feedback is approximately 60 days after possession of their home. Drive-by studies of new home move-ins show that it takes approximately six-to-eight weeks for a homeowner to get relatively situated in their new home. This timing allows the customer to assess the entire experience from purchase, to delivery conditions and into the post-delivery customer service. They can now thoughtfully reflect on the homebuying/building experience and the people who shepherded them (or not) through the process. This slight delay in survey timing also allows the customer to be less stressed (after settling in) and thus more open to sharing both rational and emotional feedback. Don't sweat the 60-day delay--one of the aforementioned studies found this 60-day feedback is an excellent predictor of the company's performance over the next 12-18 months.

For a VOC/customer satisfaction survey to be fully-effective it also has to accurately identify sources of customer *dissatisfaction.* Identifying the sources of customer dissatisfaction (i.e. inaccurate sales promises, poor in-process communications, incomplete home at delivery, individual or teamwork breakdowns, etc.) provides the prescription for future performance improvement. If you don't know what or where the customer pain is then you're only guessing. And as complex as homebuilding is, you can guess wrong many more times than correctly. Keep it simple--let the customer feedback guide you in your personnel and/or process improvements. From experience, I can tell you that you'll sleep better at night knowing you're working with accurate, honest and objective customer feedback. We all feel good when we know what we do well and even better when we are aware of our potential improvement opportunities.

The Third Leg: Building a Customer-Centric Team

If you are producing great homes and have a customer-satisfaction plan, why are you not experiencing higher customer satisfaction yet? The answer is easy. Teamwork!

Much has been written in many industries about the importance of teamwork, but it is particularly powerful in homebuilding. In fact, a recent study of 4,000 homeowners found homebuilding companies with *Very Good* teamwork ratings achieved a nearly impossible 100% Willingness to Refer, while a *Very Poor* teamwork rating yields just 14% WTR! This suggests that homebuilding puts a staggering 685% premium on teamwork and higher referral sales is its frothy dividend. So how do you build and measure teamwork in your organization?

1. Hire Team Players

When choosing your employees, look for people who already demonstrate a comfort with teamwork. People who choose to participate in team sports, band, theater or choral groups or who are involved in community, political or volunteer work understand the value of working as a team. When asking questions during the interview, it's important to listen for comments which focus on team efforts rather than just personal successes. Also, are they willing to be personally accountable for mistakes or do they blame others? To build a great team, you need the raw material--great employees.

2. Clearly Define each Team Member's Role

Scopes of work aren't just for trade partners. Every employee needs a map detailing expectations and measurable standards of performance. Once you've created your ideal customer-experience plan, executing it means every member of your remarkable, team-oriented staff knows exactly what to do to meet those customer goals. To make this happen, management must regularly train, reinforce and coach team members on their individual and team roles and responsibilities. You can't hold employees accountable for their performance unless they have been given the tools and training to do their jobs well.

3. **Use Specific Indicators to Measure Performance**

As you create each team member's scope of work, it's critical also to define measurable goals and ways to measure their success at meeting those goals. These Key Performance Indicators need to be identified for every member of your team. If you can't identify what each team member is specifically required to do, or a measurement for their achievement, then you either have a sloppy scope of work or an unnecessary role. Performance indicators should be specific at the corporate, community and individual levels. As discussed earlier, the best individual and team performance mechanism is a third party, well-designed, Voice-of-the-Customer program.

4. **Practice Performance Monitoring and Feedback**

If your surveys end up stacked in a corner or just summarized with a glance, don't bother. Lip service to customer service is worse than no attention at all. Measuring alone isn't enough. You have to look for patterns, monitor trends, keep everyone aware of any problems which arise and fix them. Frequent monitoring is critical for teamwork success. Just like in sports, people play better when there are game clocks, scoreboards, streaming statistics and replays. And as players will respond to coaches, team members will listen to managers when they react to critical issues arising in customer feedback. One role of every leader/coach is to determine both a short-and-long-term cost/benefit analysis of every member's productivity and recognize their individual contributions to the team's goals.

5. **Embrace Constant Communication**

Whether you're playing beach volleyball or soccer or building homes, smart teams huddle up before, during and after every game. Some of the best homebuilders find holding short stand-up meetings every morning helps everyone stay in touch with daily rhythms and share company updates. Communication is essential to teamwork. And it's not just teamwork or customer satisfaction which is affected by strong communication. Employee satisfaction surveys consistently show that communication is one of the most important workplace characteristics. Study after study shows happy employees lead to happy customers. Don't rely on email and other digital tools. An over-reliance on digital communication by management or staff can actually be counterproductive on the teamwork scoreboard. The preferred medium is face-to-face.

6. **Understand that the Customer Really Does Know Best**

A Voice-of-the-Customer tool provides homebuilders with constant, realistic and insightful information on what your homebuyers value about your homes and your homebuying process. They'll also be bluntly honest when you've let them down. No consultant in the world can give you better information, and no marketing plan is as powerful as a current homeowner who personally recommends you to a potential homebuyer. Thirty years in the business and lots of analytics have shown that VOC is one of the critical metrics to monitor. Ninety-seven percent of all customers are reasonable people and only about 3% are impossible to please. If more than 3% of your customers are sharing negative feedback or ratings, then your company has a real opportunity to improve its customer satisfaction position. Ignore those voices at your peril.

The End Result:

Now, sit down on that sturdy three-legged stool you just built and enjoy. NOTHING is as personally and financially rewarding as selling great homes, creating enthusiastic homeowners and leading a customer-centric, motivated and happy staff. This truly is a true win:win:win scenario.

Questions:

What are your biggest sources of revenue slippage?

What is your current referral sales revenue as a percentage of total revenue and how much are you missing?

What is your customer experience plan and how is it measured?

Take a Moment...

Understand the customer satisfaction hierarchy of needs.

Define the customer experience plan and teach individual and team roles.

Implement an accurate Voice-of-the-Customer (VOC) program to identify customer satisfaction strengths and improvement opportunities.

Hire team players, coach them well and give them regular VOC feedback.

Develop a referral sales mindset and defined strategy.

Set a referral sales goal at 30-40%, then measure, report and celebrate them regularly.

The Final Close

I want to thank all of the industry professionals who have taken time to share their expertise with me and with all of you who are reading this book. It is my sincere hope that their years of varied experiences in the New Home Sales and Marketing arena will benefit you regardless of your position, title or experience level. Anyone in this great industry will surely capture many *gold nuggets* from these *golden colleagues* of mine!

It is particularly fitting that this final chapter is about *Closing*, since in the end, that is ultimately what the chapters in this book represent...*creating the relationship and closing the sale.*

We've all heard the quote, "Life is a journey, not a destination." If we relate this quote to our industry, the destination is the *closing and referral* while the journey is the *sales process*, which is everyone's friend.

There are a variety of specialized subjects presented in these chapters but the common thread they share is that each topic illustrates an important and integral part of the journey--the *process*. Each chapter teaches us something about the value of every person's role in the sales process and what we can all do to ensure both our personal and company's success, be it in marketing, recruiting or online presence, just to name a few. Take note of the recurring theme whether implied or stated directly, surrounding the importance of the customer's journey, that it be the most positive and rewarding experience possible. The quality of the experience needs to be as equally important as the quality of the home you build. Do these following statements sound familiar? They should...your experts said it best!

- "You are there to help your customer see what can change in their world."
- "How do you deliver a world-class customer experience? Thrill and delight your buyers with an unparalleled buying experience."
- "One way to earn trust is by having a clear, consistent, recognizable brand."
- "Build the relationship first. The quality of your relationship with your customer is commensurate with the quality of the experience for all involved."
- "Understand that the customer really does know best."

My closing sentiments to you, the reader, are that you take and apply the information presented in these chapters to ensure you are doing your absolute best to promote the success of your company, the positive experience for your customer and most of all, your own personal growth and success in this amazing industry!

28756892R00061

Made in the USA
Columbia, SC
24 October 2018